This book is dedicated to my dear Brother David —

my teacher, friend, and mentor.

TABLE OF CONTENTS

Foreword

By Gary Fiedel

Fifteen years ago, Brother David Steindl-Rast asked me and several friends to help him create a website that would feature his and others' teachings about gratefulness.

Brother David is a world-renowned Benedictine monk who has spent much of his life writing and teaching about gratefulness. We formed a nonprofit organization, A Network for Grateful Living (ANG*L), that has both an online and offline mission. Online we launched the website Gratefulness.org on Thanksgiving 2000. The purpose is to inspire and help folks to live a more grateful life and enjoy the many benefits that go with it.

Since then, more than 20 million visitors from more than 200 countries have come to Gratefulness.org for inspiration, solace, and to learn about living gratefully. The website is packed with features toward that purpose, including articles by many of the world's spiritual leaders, an inspiring word for the day, beautiful e-cards, positive news, a unique light-a-candle feature, and more, including hundreds of videos, interviews, and lectures by Brother David.

I personally have been profoundly affected by Brother David's teachings. When I first met him 30 years ago, I hadn't really thought about gratefulness much. I soon became a dedicated practitioner. In my experience, when I endeavor to remember to be grateful, I become more grateful, and life is better. The resources on the website have been a source of great inspiration for me. I've found the grateful "practices" to be particularly useful in building my grateful muscle.

But I wanted a place to go "offline" where I could continue working on my practice. With Brother David's encouragement, I put together a team, and we have adapted the practices here to book form. He came up with a simple but powerful way to approach a grateful practice: "STOP – LOOK – GO." We hope that this book will become a special companion to you as you move through your life. By following the directions in each practice, you will actually feel more grateful. The act of writing and reflecting on the various aspects of the gifts we are given has been proven to literally increase our ability to feel grateful more often.

Brother David often says that if more people were grateful, the world would actually begin to change for the better. You can't be grateful and hateful; you can't be grateful and selfish. Gratefulness confers a host of benefits for the individual and for the world.

A favorite practice of mine comes directly from a quote by Brother David: "We are never more than one grateful thought away from peace of heart." When I turn my attention to feeling grateful, I feel happy and blessed. My mind is at peace.

The practices in this book were created to cultivate gratitude and the joy, kindness, and well-being that gratitude brings. My wish for you is that your life is happier and better as you learn to practice living gratefully.

Gratefully yours,

Gary Fiedel, *Cofounder, Gratefulness.org and A Network for Grateful Living (ANG*L)*

Introduction: The ABCs of Gratefulness

by Brother David Steindl-Rast

Enthusiasm is too weak a word for the thrill I feel about this *Practice Workbook*. My heart overflows with gratitude to my dear friends, Gary Fiedel, Karie Jacobson and Candice Fuhrman for their nine-month labor that gave birth to this promising baby.

It takes practice to achieve gratefulness. Without a doubt, Stop – Look – Go will help innumerable seekers to find the joy of grateful living through the practical instructions it offers. In fact, it might inspire readers to invent their own additional gratefulness practices.

One such practice that I use sometimes – say, in my dentist's waiting-room – I call the ABCs of Grateful Living: I go through the alphabet and note for each letter the first word that comes to my mind. Then, I try to make a connection between that word and my practice of grateful living. It's a kind of game I play with myself.

Forewords and introductions tend to be boring. Let's instead play this game. I promise to honestly take the first word I think of. Well, here we go:

A – AMAZEMENT

I mean that vibrant sense of wonder that triggers gratefulness. Mary Oliver expressed it so well:

> "When it's over, I want to say: all my life
> I was a bride married to amazement.
> I was the bridegroom, taking the world into my arms."

B – BEAUTY

Not prettiness, but beauty as of a thunderstorm gripping my heart with a sense of mystery – this is the deepest root of gratefulness.

C – CHERRIES

Shiny red, big, and plump cherries, or even the tiny wild ones, so sweet on my tongue, are for me, as long as I can remember, an image of all that nature's abundance bestows and our heart leaps to receive with gratitude.

D – DEATH

Living and dying belong together. Learning to live is learning to die. By learning to live gratefully, we learn to die peacefully.

E – EARTH

What a gift is this planet of ours! Gary Snyder speaks of it as the Earth Household. Earthworms, sunflowers, humans, lions, supernovas – all members of this household are gifts to one another. Gratitude of each to each – simply for being there – holds everything together.

F – FIREFLIES

Or should I have said Fireworks? I'm thrilled by both. Once on a Fourth of July I heard the sound of fireworks and went out to see them. But a hill blocked my view. Instead, I noticed thousands of fireflies in the meadow around me. Aren't surprise and gratitude almost synonyms?

G – GIVING

There are three levels of giving: Giving away makes you free. Giving thanks makes you joyful. *For*giving, the most intense level of giving, makes you fully human.

H – HANDS and HEART

Among all the wonderful things that human hands can do, giving gifts is the noblest activity. But, as an African proverb says: "It is the heart that gives, the hands merely let go."

I – I AM

I have not brought about, or bought, or made myself. From the start I discover myself as a given – one big gift given to myself. What else should I make of my life but one big thanksgiving?

J – JOURNEY

Life is a journey. Grateful living turns life into a pilgrimage. The success of a journey depends on reaching the goal. But on a pilgrimage every step is the goal.

K – KNEELING

Gratitude makes us want to kneel from sheer delight. Again, Mary Oliver puts it perfectly:
"I don't know exactly what a prayer is.
I do know how to pay attention,
how to fall down into the grass,
how to kneel down in the grass,
how to be idle and blessed,
how to stroll through the fields,
which is what I have been doing all day.
Tell me, what else should I have done?
Doesn't everything die at last, and too soon?
Tell me, what is it you plan to do
with your one wild and precious life?"

L – LEAVE-TAKING

The more we become aware that every moment of life is a leave-taking, the more we learn to appreciate life gratefully.

M – MUSIC and MYSTERY

We cannot grasp music intellectually; yet, we can understand music, if it, in turn, "grabs" us. Likewise the Great Mystery that some call God: We cannot wrap our mind around it, but we can gratefully allow it to embrace us – and thus understand.

N – NOW

The greatest gift of all is the present moment. All spiritual practices lead to living gratefully in the Now.

O – OPPORTUNITY

The gift within every gift is opportunity. We cannot be grateful for everything. But we can be grateful every moment for the opportunities it gives us – if not to enjoy, then to learn, to grow, to serve.

P – POTHOLES
Potholes in the road give us the opportunity to slow down. That's a great gift.

Q – QUESTIONS
I'm grateful for questions, especially unanswered ones; they keep me alert.

R – RAIN
Makes plants grow; gratitude makes human relationships grow.

S – SIMPLICITY
Grateful people live simply – so that others may simply live.

T – TRUST
Life inevitably brings anxieties. If we resist anxiety because of fear – a lack of trust -- we get stuck. Trust in life lets us move through the narrow passage of anxiety into a new birth.

U – UMBRELLA
Evening rain tapping on my yellow umbrella: The "little" gifts of life, how big they are!

V – VOTING
Yes, I know, voting is made difficult for the poor and the system is riddled with injustice. All the more, I stop and look for the opportunity to promote justice, and go voting.

W – WIKIPEDIA
Sharing all knowledge for free! Do we support this project as it deserves? We can transform giving money as payment into giving money as thanks.

X – Gratitude is an "x"
A multiplication sign: It multiplies our joy as many times as we "stop, look, and go!"

Y – YOU
We can learn to say "you" gratefully. Without you, the very word "I" would make no sense. In a love poem e.e. cummings writes: "i am through you so i."

Z – ZAP! You are it!
Now it's your turn to play this ABC Gratefulness Game.

PART 1

Foundations of Gratefulness

Chapter 1: STOP – LOOK – GO: A Basic Gratefulness Practice[1]

If, each day, we could perform a basic daily gratefulness practice, it would be enough to positively impact our lives and the world around us. That is the best thing about having a foundational practice to which we can always return; just because it is simple does not mean it has simple results.

This practice can be done anytime, anywhere, and as often as you want. You might choose to engage in this practice in a more formal way at the same time each day.

In this workbook, we will be using a basic three-step gratefulness practice as our foundation. This technique, gratefully borrowed from Brother David Steindl-Rast, is called simply "STOP – LOOK – GO." It works beautifully on its own and can be done daily. You can also use this technique as the basis for more specific meditations, which we will be describing in later chapters.

The STOP – LOOK – GO technique is summed up in the following three steps:

STOP become present, awake, aware, receptive

LOOK notice, observe, consider, have a direct experience

GO acknowledge, take action, do something with the opportunity and awareness which gratefulness offers you

Before you move on to this first practice, please read the following excerpt from Brother David's essay, "Awake, Aware, Alert," in which he describes the basis of the STOP – LOOK – GO technique.

---

[1] Adapted from "Awake, Aware, Alert" by Brother David Steindl-Rast, on Gratefulness.org at www.gratefulness.org/resource/awake-aware-and-alert/ and from "A Basic Daily Gratefulness Practice," on Gratefulness.org at http://www.gratefulness.org/resource/basic-daily-gratefulness-practice/

To begin with, we never start to be grateful unless we wake up. Wake up to what?
To surprise. As long as nothing surprises us, we walk through life in a daze. We need to
practice waking up to surprise. I suggest using this simple question as a kind of alarm
clock: "Isn't this surprising?"

"Yes, indeed!" will be the correct answer, no matter when and where and under what
circumstances you ask this question. After all, isn't it surprising that there is anything at all,
rather than nothing? Ask yourself at least twice a day, "Isn't this surprising?" and you will
soon be more awake to the surprising world in which we live. Surprise may provide a jolt,
enough to wake us up and to stop taking everything for granted.

It helps me to review my own practice of gratefulness by applying these three basic
steps I learned as a boy for crossing an intersection: "STOP, LOOK, GO."

Before going to bed, I glance back over the day and ask myself: Did I STOP and
allow myself to be surprised? Or did I trudge on in a daze? Was I too busy to wake up
to surprise?

And once I stopped, did I LOOK for the opportunity of that moment? Or did I allow
the circumstances to distract me from the gift within the gift? (This tends to happen when the
gift's wrappings are not attractive.) Most times, the opportunity is to enjoy.

And finally, was I alert enough to GO after it, to avail myself fully of the opportunity
offered to me?

There are times, I must admit, when stopping at night to review my day, I look back
and realize with regret how much I missed. Not only was I less grateful on those non-stop
days, I was less alive, somehow numb. Other days may be just as busy, but I do remember to
STOP; on those days, I even accomplish more because stopping breaks up the routine.

But unless I also LOOK, the stopping alone will not make my day a truly happy one;
what difference does it make that I am not on an express train but on a local if I'm not aware
of the scenery outside the windows? On some days, I find in my nightly review that I stopped
and I looked, but not with alertness. Just yesterday, I found a huge moth on the sidewalk;
I did stop long enough to put it in a safe spot on the lawn, just a foot away, but I didn't
crouch down to spend time with this marvelous creature. Only faintly did I remember,
at night, those iridescent eyes on the grayish brown wings. My day was diminished by
this failure to stay long enough with this surprise gift to deeply look at it and to savor its
beauty gratefully.

My simple recipe for a joyful day is this: STOP and wake up; LOOK and be aware
of what you see; then GO on with all the alertness you can muster for the opportunity the
moment offers. Looking back in the evening, on a day on which I made these three steps
over and over, is like looking at an apple orchard heavy with fruit.

– Brother David Steindl-Rast

Now, try this practice for yourself. If you want to get better at something, you practice. As you practice, you will get better. As we mentioned earlier, you'll be using this basic practice as the foundation to explore specific facets of gratefulness in your life in later chapters. No matter what facets you explore, remember that you can always come back to the simplicity of this foundational practice.

Practice: STOP – LOOK – GO

STOP whatever you are doing and devote your full attention to being still or slowing down. If it helps, you can close your eyes. Become conscious of your breath; follow a complete inhale–exhale cycle with your full awareness. Bring your awareness to the gift of the present moment and allow yourself to soften into it.

LOOK at what life is offering you right now. Consider the invitation to feel grateful for what you already have in your life. Expand the feeling and let it grow inside you.

Next, preserve your reflections. Research and experience say that writing down grateful thoughts can be very helpful.

GO and write down at least three things that you are grateful for in the space below. Your answers do not have to be grand or complicated. Some of the most meaningful things to acknowledge are those we commonly take for granted. Examples include: our loved ones, our senses, having a place to live, the ability to learn and grow, a pet, food, a friend, a part of nature.

_____

_____

_____

Now, go one step further, and think of each of these things as a gift as opposed to a given. We can elevate anything in our lives – especially the routine and most common parts of our lives – by receiving it with the same kind of gratitude that we would receive an unexpected gift.

It can be a powerful part of the practice to actually begin each acknowledgement of gratitude with the words, "I am grateful for the gift of..."

Above, you wrote down three things you are grateful to have in your life. Now try expressing your gratitude in terms of receiving a gift. Using the same three things you expressed gratitude for above, complete three sentences, starting with the phrase:

"I am grateful for the gift of..."

_____

_____

_____

If you are in a place where you can comfortably speak out loud, try saying these phrases out loud as well. Notice how this changes your feelings about the things you are grateful for.

Finally, allow your feelings to spill over into expressing grateful sentiments to those around you. Choose one person today to thank for something ordinary or extraordinary.

Take a risk to acknowledge kindness. Honor someone who is being cooperative.

Commend generosity. Praise courage. Appreciate authenticity. Start a grateful ripple. Whatever you choose to do, make sure to notice the difference it makes. Come back to this workbook, and write down what you experienced by thanking someone.

Who did you thank today?

_____

_____

_____

What were the results?

_____

_____

_____

Congratulations! You have just practiced gratefulness in your life. You have even started your own written record of gratitude. The next chapter will guide you through a more specific exercise and, we hope, kindle new awareness and appreciation for aspects of life you may normally take for granted.

> _What can anyone give you greater than_
> _now, starting here, right in this room,_
> _when you turn around?_
> — William Stafford

Chapter 2: Treasure Chest of Life[2]

One of the most amazing gifts of being human is the capacity we have for choice: the miracle of all miracles. Consciously or unconsciously, we have the ability to choose where to put our attention within each moment. We can choose to respond to each moment by creating, inspiring, imagining, doing, or otherwise actively engaging with it. Or, we can react to each moment through withdrawal and careful protection.

Because our innate impulse is survival, we are mostly on automatic radar for anything that might endanger us. This means that our default attitude, as human beings, tends to be fear of what could go wrong. Accordingly, we most often operate in the react mode, rather than the respond mode. This is a natural way of being in the world, as our instinct holds safety as primary – a natural instinct, but a limiting one. When we react to events instinctively, rather than deliberately choosing our response, we limit the potential of the moment.

Living day-to-day in a mostly reactive mode means feeling less alive, flat, more anxious, and not very engaged in life. Responding is a lot more fulfilling and satisfying than reacting.

The question then becomes how do we learn to be more responsive versus reactive on a day-to-day basis? The answer is simple: practice! There are many ways to practice. Here, we offer one that is a ton of fun and very satisfying. It is called it the "Treasure Chest of Life" practice.

---

[2] Adapted from "Treasure Chest of Life" Practice by Chuck Roppel, on Gratefulness.org at http://www.gratefulness.org/resource/treasure-chest-practice/

Practice: Treasure Chest of Life

STOP

Set aside at least 15 minutes to do this practice. You will also need to get a few things ready before you start: a pen, some paper, and your "Treasure Chest." Your "chest" can be a simple cardboard box, a vase, an old fish tank, or any other safe, special place to which you have ready access.

LOOK

Begin by reflecting on your earliest memories of the sweet moments in your life and write down each one, as a brief phrase. For example, one person remembered being about seven years old, walking out in the yard in Kentucky in April when the red bud trees were in full bloom. It was breathtaking. His one-liner for that event was simply: "Red bud trees at seven years old."

In the space below, write down three one-line descriptions of sweet moments in your life.

_____

_____

_____

GO

Take your time, gradually working your way through each decade of your life, noting all the sweet moments, small and large. Make the list as long as you can and cut up each one-liner into a single strip of paper. Fold each one and place it in your "treasure chest."

Keep creating new lists over time. Eventually, you will have hundreds of recorded memories in your chest of treasures. Each day as you pass by your "Treasure Chest," pull out a memory, and notice how your face relaxes, your heart opens, you are more present and there is more fullness and appreciation for your life.

You see, we get what we look for. If we look for the treasure, we will find a treasure. If we look for what's wrong, we will find what's wrong.

This is how we learn responsive living: by choosing how to focus our attention. This conscious, grateful living practice is simple, takes little time, and is immensely gratifying.

If you have enjoyed this practice, share it with a friend. And may your whole life become a chest of treasures.

Chapter 3: Mindful Breathing for Grateful Living[3]

Many of the practices in this book begin with a basic breathing exercise, and in fact, mindful breathing on its own is a fantastic way to cultivate gratefulness. By simply focusing on breathing in and out with full awareness, you can focus your thoughts away from distractions and stress, bringing yourself into the present moment. Being in the present moment leads to gratefulness.

Mindful breathing is good for the body as well. Author Chade-Meng Tan recently wrote a piece for the *Harvard Business Review* titled, "Just 6 Seconds of Mindfulness Can Make You More Effective."[4] In it, he details why mindful breathing is effective at bringing calm to both body and mind. "The physiological reason is that breaths taken mindfully tend to be slow and deep, which stimulates the vagus nerve, activating the parasympathetic nervous system.

It lowers stress, reduces heart rate and blood pressure, and calms you down." Tan also points out that even one mindful breath can help focus and prepare your mind when you need it — for instance, just before entering a business meeting.

> *Remember to breathe.*
> *It is after all, the secret of life.*
> — Gregory Maguire

The more you practice mindful breathing, the more effective you will be at helping calm yourself even when you have only a few seconds to do a mindful breathing exercise. And, by practicing mindful breathing in moments of relative calm, you will get better at practicing it under stressful situations and in spite of outward distractions. We ask that you set aside a full fifteen minutes for the following practice.

---

[3] Adapted from "Mindful Breathing" from the Greater Good In Action website at http://ggia.berkeley.edu/practice/mindful_breathing

[4] Chade-Meng Tan, "Just 6 Seconds of Mindfulness Can Make You More Effective." https://hbr.org/2015/12/just-6-seconds-of-mindfulness-can-make-you-more-effective

Practice: Mindful Breathing

STOP

Set aside fifteen minutes to do this exercise regularly. Experts believe a regular practice of mindful breathing can make it easier to do in difficult situations.

LOOK

Close your eyes. Focus your attention on your breath, the inhale and the exhale. You can do this while standing, but ideally you'll be sitting or even lying in a comfortable position. Notice how your breathing so often takes care of itself...just breath moving itself through you — keeping you alive — just keeping you alive. Commit to not taking this miracle for granted.

GO

Take a few, very deep breaths — all the way out and all the way in. Sometimes, especially when trying to calm yourself in a stressful moment, it might help to start by taking an exaggerated breath: a deep inhale through your nostrils (three seconds), hold your breath (two seconds), and a long exhale through your mouth (four seconds). Then, simply observe each breath without trying to adjust it; it may help to focus on the rise and fall of your chest or the sensation through your nostrils. As you do so, you may find that your mind wanders, distracted by thoughts or bodily sensations. That's okay. Just notice that this is happening and gently bring your attention back to your breath.

If you need to practice your basic breathing more, do this exercise daily for at least a week. It can help to set aside a designated time and place for this exercise; it can be a great way to start your day. It can also help to practice mindful breathing when you're feeling particularly stressed or anxious.

What Does A Grateful Brain Look Like?*

A team at the University of Southern California has shed light on the neural nuts and bolts of gratitude in a study, offering insights into the complexity of this social emotion and how it relates to other cognitive processes.

The researchers found that grateful brains showed enhanced activity in two primary regions: the anterior cingulate cortex (ACC) and the medial prefrontal cortex (mPFC). These areas have been previously associated with emotional processing, interpersonal bonding and rewarding social interactions, moral judgment, and the ability to understand the mental states of others.

---

* Adam Hoffman, article for the Greater Good Science Center. A more detailed description of this can be found at the National Center for Biotechnology Information site in the article, "The effects of gratitude expression on neural activity." by Kini P., Wong J., McInnis S., Gabana N., Brown JW.

Chapter 4: Three Good Things [5]

We tend to adapt to the good things and people in our lives, taking them for granted.

As a result, we often overlook everyday beauty and goodness — a kind gesture from

a stranger, say, or the warmth of our heater

on a chilly morning. In the process, we

frequently miss opportunities for happiness

and connection.

> *Man only likes to count his troubles;*
> *he doesn't calculate his happiness.*
> — Fyodor Dostoyevsky

This practice guards against those tendencies. By remembering and listing three

positive things that have happened in your day — and considering what caused them

— you tune into the sources of goodness in your life. It's a habit that can change the

emotional tone of your life, replacing feelings of disappointment or entitlement with

those of gratitude — which may be why this practice is associated with significant

increases in happiness.

[5] From the exercise "Three Good Things," from the Greater Good In Action Website at
http://ggia.berkeley.edu/practice/three-good-things

Practice: Three Good Things

STOP

You will need to set aside a few minutes every day for three days to write in this workbook. To make this exercise part of your daily routine, some find that writing before bed is helpful. Create a plan.

LOOK

As you go about your day, just the knowledge that you'll be on the lookout for good things will in itself probably make you more aware of them. When something pleasurable does happen, take another little extra moment to take notice of it. You'll be writing a description later, so you'll need a few details to write down!

GO

In the charts provided, starting on the next page, write down one thing that went well for you each day, and provide an explanation for why it went well. It is important to create a physical record of your items by writing them down; it is not enough simply to do this exercise in your head. The items can be relatively small in importance (e.g., "my loved one or coworker made the coffee today") or relatively large (e.g., "I earned a big promotion").

> *The best way to pay for a lovely moment is to enjoy it.*
> — Richard Bach

Please read through this <u>*explanation of the categories in the chart*</u> *before you start:*

Title | Give the event a title (e.g., "coworker complimented my work on a project")

Description | Write down exactly what happened in as much detail as possible, including what you did or said and, if others were involved, what they did or said. Include how this event made you feel at the time and how this event made you feel later (including now, as you remember it). Use whatever writing style you please, and do not worry about perfect grammar and spelling. Use as much detail as you'd like.

Cause | Explain why you think the event came to pass. Reflecting on the cause of the event may help attune you to the deeper sources of goodness in your life, fostering a mindset of gratitude. The cause is often the kind of thing that "goes without saying," and may feel a bit obvious as you write it. But the simple act of writing it down can be illuminating in unexpected ways. For instance, take the case of "my loved one [or coworker] made the coffee today." Perhaps in the description you already described the overall pleasantness of this small event. As the cause, you might write, "She thought we would enjoy a warm cup of coffee." Writing the cause in this case highlights a deliberately kind act and rounds out the description of the GOOD THING event.

GOOD THING — Day One:

TITLE
DESCRIPTION
CAUSE

GOOD THING — Day Two:

TITLE
DESCRIPTION
CAUSE

GOOD THING — Day Three:

TITLE
DESCRIPTION
CAUSE

How do you feel after three days of this practice? By giving you the space to focus on the positive, this practice teaches you to notice, remember, and savor the better things in life. It may prompt you to pay closer attention to positive events down the road and engage in them more fully — both in the moment and later on, when you can reminisce and share these experiences with others.

The Science of Gratitude *

The scientific study of the effects of gratitude is flourishing. Research partners Robert A. Emmons and Michael McCullough are among those who have conducted many such studies, with striking results.

Emmons and McCullough found that when people regularly work on cultivating gratitude, they experience a variety of measurable benefits.

Participants in their studies reported higher levels of positive emotions, such as joy, pleasure, optimism and happiness, and feeling more alive and awake.

They also experienced health benefits, such as stronger immune systems, lower blood pressure, improved sleep, and fewer aches and pains, and they exercised more and took better care of their health.

---

* Robert Emmons, Ph.D., University of California, Davis. Michael McCullough, University of Miami. Partially adapted from Robert Emmons' article, "Pay it Forward," on the Greater Good Science Center website.

Chapter 5: Gratefulness for Sufficiency[6]

> *Give thanks for a little and you will find a lot.* — The Hausa of Nigeria

A sense of scarcity and urgency is commonplace for many of us. Often, habits of mind and behavior keep us on the treadmill of "more is better." When we are busy unconsciously rushing towards more, as *The Soul of Money* author Lynne Twist notes, we rush right over/past "enough" and do not even notice it...like an inconvenient speed bump.

> *The store was closed, so I went home and hugged what I own.*
> — Brooks Palmer

But when we are in touch with "enough-ness," we become less susceptible to cultural norms of complaint, envy, scarcity, comparison, and insatiability.

The following practices are devoted to creating a new set of norms for your daily life — a sense of sufficiency, spaciousness, and appreciation.

---

[6] Adapted from "Appreciating Sufficiency" on Gratefulness.org at www.gratefulness.org/resource/appreciating-sufficiency/

Practice: Gratefulness for Sufficiency

STOP whatever you are doing and devote your full attention to being still or slowing down. If it helps, close your eyes. Become conscious of your breath—the breathing itself. Follow one complete inhale-exhale cycle with your attention. Notice how simply and exquisitely you are nourished and renewed by the flow of air in your lungs. Bring your awareness to the present moment, and allow yourself to soften into it.

LOOK at the place where you live. Notice that you have a place to live. Try to see it through a fresh lens, through new, unaccustomed eyes. Imagine someone coming to visit your residence who has a great deal less than you do (no matter what you have, there are always people who have less).

> *Naming and appreciation of the gifts that surround us creates a sense of satisfaction, a feeling of "enoughness" that is an antidote to the societal messages that drill into our spirits, telling us we must have more. Practicing contentment is a radical act in a consumption-driven society.* — Dr. Robin Wall Kimmerer

Imagine yourself showing the person where you live — taking them through each space in your home. This exercise can add immediate perspective to how you see your surroundings.

Where did you take your imaginary visitor?

_____

Now, try focusing specifically on the kitchen — the place where you prepare food. Allow yourself to imagine that the room was completely empty or that this room did not exist at all. See empty cupboards, counters, and drawers in your mind's eye.

What would change in your life if you did not have what you have in your kitchen?

_____

_____

_____

What does this place offer you and others in your life?

_____

_____

_____

GO

Notice what you need and love in your kitchen. Appreciate each thing: the faucet, a stove, spoons, etc. Now choose three things to express your appreciation for with a concrete action. Draw a heart on beloved items with an erasable pen. Or put a heart sticker on it. Or a Post-it note with the word "gift."

What creative actions did you take to express your gratitude for the things in your kitchen? Which items did you choose?

_____

_____

_____

Next, think about what you may have more of than you truly need. Are there clothes that you no longer wear? Books overflowing the shelves? Boxes of "junk" in your garage?

> *Not what we have, but what we enjoy, constitutes our abundance.*
> — Epicurus

Write down at least one thing that you have in surplus. If you can, write down three things. Think creatively. Things that are "junk" to you, such as glasses with an expired prescription, or an old cell phone from which you've upgraded, are surplus items that you no longer need.

_____

_____

_____

Wherever you notice "more than I need," keep a bag or box and begin putting things in there to give to others who might love/need them more than you do. Put a bag or box in each room for a period of time so that as you notice "surplus," you can share it. Look into formally sharing bigger items that are used less often with neighbors or friends — a bicycle, lawnmower, and laundry appliances. Learn about and contact Freecycle.

Notice the enoughness of your life in as many ways as you can. Allow feelings of scarcity to move away in favor of a sense of sufficiency — appreciating what is yours to appreciate. Wherever there is enough or more-than-enough, let yourself experience this as a gift.

Complete this chapter by writing about your experience in your workbook. What impressed you the most? How did thinking about what you have from a new perspective change your feelings about enoughness? What did enoughness feel like? How is it different from the feeling of needing more?

Chapter 6: The Gift of Water[7]

All life is dependent on water. What could be more fundamental to our existence than water? Yet, most of us in the Western world take it for granted.

As we grieve over worldwide droughts, contaminated drinking water, and oil spills in our oceans, our awareness of how precious water is becomes clearer and stronger. We can practice gratefulness by acknowledging the gift of water in our lives.

> *The supreme good is like water, which nourishes all things without trying to.*
> — Lao-Tzu

If you try to describe water in a general way, you may find your words sounding strangely spiritual. It's all around us, yet also deep within us, sustaining every cell of our bodies. It cleanses and heals us. All life depends on it. Is this really the same stuff with which you brush your teeth every day, with which kids fill their squirt guns, with which you scrub your sticky dishes? Maybe we need to see water with a new appreciation.

[7] Adapted from "Water Blessings" on Gratefulness.org at http://gratefulness.org/resource/water-blessings/

and "Practice: Gratefulness for Water," formerly on Gratefulness.org

Practice: Gratefulness for Water

STOP

Find a quiet place, and concentrate on your breathing until you feel yourself relax. Now, imagine that you find yourself walking on a trail in the woods, just before dawn, after the first snow of the year. The oak leaves crunching beneath your feet let snow nestle in their crinkled bowls; the pines bow slightly in their new fleece. You reach up and pinch a little snow from their branches, and the freshness of its cool taste on your tongue startles you. Not far away you can hear a not-yet-frozen waterfall flowing with the full force of recent autumn rains.

Where is water not to be found in this woods world? It adorns the branches and runs through their vessels. It forms fleeting clouds with each breath you exhale, and with each inhalation you can feel in your mouth how you yourself are made almost entirely of water. It runs through the streams that lead to the source of the water you drink. You could not live without its physical sustenance, but neither could you be truly alive without its beauty.

> *Water flows from high in the mountains; water runs deep in the Earth. Miraculously, water comes to us, and sustains all life.*
> — Thich Nhat Hanh

LOOK

Perhaps you live far from the forest. Perhaps you're in the desert, surrounded by cacti and sand. Perhaps you live in a big city, where you depend on pipes and bottles to bring you water. Whatever your source of water, it is certain that you do have a source, for without water, you would not be alive.

Pour yourself a glass of water. Look at the clear beauty of this life-sustaining gift. This is a glass of water, fit for you to drink. It is not polluted with mud or sand; it is not salty and undrinkable, as seawater is.

> *Water is life's mater and matrix, mother and medium.*
> — Albert Szent-Gyorgyi

GO

Now, lift the glass to your mouth and drink the water with your full awareness. You may wish to close your eyes to savor the sensation, or you may want to admire the crystal water as it refreshes your tongue and throat.

To further accentuate your new awareness of the gift of water, write down two reasons why you are grateful for water.

I am grateful for water because:

_____

_____

_____

How do you suppose we humans, as a species, are thanking water for keeping us alive? Allow yourself to think about the 1.1 billion people who don't have access to safe drinking water, or the fact that 50 percent of our rivers are seriously polluted These stark facts are a far cry from the simplicity of your walk in the woods with which this practice began. Where do we start to redress these imbalances?

We might begin by translating into action the water metaphor of a Sufi master, Hazrat Inayat Khan:

"It is a patient pursuit to bring water from the depth of the ground;
one has to deal with much mud in digging before one reaches the
water of life."

We will not bring about change in any simple, single act. But if we steadily dig away at the problem, without losing heart, we can begin to reach our goal. And working together speeds the process immeasurably.

You may want to take a look at a listing of worldwide organizations, to let yourself be inspired by the myriad ways in which dedicated human beings address the water needs of earth. You might even want to volunteer your help or use these ideas to get a project started in your own backyard. There are many groups that, each in their own way, work for education, aid, and research to preserve the precious gift of water.

We have plunged into our gratefulness for water from two angles: observing how valuable it is to us yet also how we need to exponentially increase our efforts to protect this life-giving resource. You have strengthened your resolve to help protect Earth's waters. You can take that resolve a step further by telling a friend about this practice.

> *What would the world be, once bereft*
> *Of wet and of wildness? Let them be left,*
> *O let them be left, wildness and wet;*
> *Long live the weeds and the wilderness yet.*
> — Gerard Manley Hopkins, "Inversnaid"

What steps did you take today to protect the Earth's waters?

_____

_____

_____

_____

_____

_____

Chapter 7: Gratefulness for the Body As It Is[8]

No matter what is/feels "wrong" with your body, there is an overwhelming amount that is perfectly right with your body at all times. Your body is, indeed, nothing short of an absolute miracle.

Allow yourself to consider these amazing facts:
- Your body produces approximately 2.5 million new red blood cells each second.
- Your heart beats around 100,000 times each and every day.
- Your lungs can take in more than 3,000 gallons of air each day.
- Your brain uses 20% of your body's oxygen and caloric intake, even though it is only about two percent of your body mass.

Often, we are simply unkind to our bodies. We criticize the way they look with a judgmental attitude, finding minuscule faults that we'd never notice on another person. We overwork them and abuse them. More often, we simply take for granted the amazing things our bodies are accomplishing every second of our lives.

Those who are dealing with chronic illness or pain often find it difficult to focus on anything but the body negatives. Yet this is the very time when it is especially important to appreciate and treasure the body. Just as you would comfort a friend who is under stress, it's good to let your body know you care. We will explore this concept more fully later on in this book. For now, just know that

> *As long as you are breathing, there is more right with your body than wrong with it.*
>
> — Jon Kabat-Zinn

when your body is struggling, perhaps even struggling to survive, there's no better time to be aware and grateful for all that it is doing.

The following practice is meant to help you focus your attention on that which serves you, on all that is intact, and to remind you that you are alive — and that life is an unconditional gift.

Now, practice appreciating your body for all that it does for you each day.

8] Adapted from "Being Grateful for The Body As It Is" on Gratefulness.org
http://www.gratefulness.org/resource/being-grateful-for-the-body-as-it-is/

Practice: Gratefulness for the Body As It Is

STOP whatever you are doing and devote your full attention to being still or slowing down in this moment. Become conscious of your breathing. Follow a complete inhale-exhale cycle with your full awareness.

Allow your body to soften wherever it is, exactly as it is. Allow yourself to open to the possibility of greater spaciousness or ease in your relationship with your experience of your body. Feel everything gently.

You may want to take a few moments to lie down, or sit, allowing your body to rest comfortably. Feel your body supported by whatever is underneath you. You may want to put your hand, or both hands, gently on your chest. Let yourself be aware of your heart beating and/or your lungs breathing.

LOOK

Allow your attention to focus on how much is happening in your body without your effort, without your having to try to make anything happen.

It is very difficult to take our attention off of physical pain or distress. The nature of distress is that it seems to want every last morsel of our attention. But it is very important for us to know that with attention, challenging sensations and experiences in the body can be dwarfed by the larger context of all that is working.

Is there one fact that stands out to you — that makes you really appreciate the gift of your body and how much it is offering you? Allow yourself to focus on one thing about your body that is working. Appreciate it with your whole awareness.

Write down three things about your body that are working and for which you feel grateful.

I am grateful for my body because:

_____

_____

_____

GO

Move throughout the next moments carrying the idea that — no matter what else is true — your body is nothing short of miraculous. You are more than any part — you are even more than the sum of your parts. Your body is alive and it is a miracle.

Whenever your mind slips into negative thoughts about your body, interrupt the pattern by saying to yourself, "I am grateful for my body." Focus on what is working.

Find a physical gesture of tenderness and care that you can offer to yourself when you get stuck in judgments about your body — such as placing your hands on your heart. This type of gesture can be filled with meaning and association. Let it be a healing reminder to your body that it is appreciated.

> *I love this body*
> *made to weather the storm*
> *in the brain, raised*
> *out of the deep smell*
> *of fish & water hyacinth,*
> *out of rapture & the first*
> *regret. I love my big hands.*
> *I love it clear down to the soft*
> *quick motor of each breath,*
> *the liver's ten kinds of desire*
> *& the kidney's lust for sugar.*
> — Yusef Komunyakaa

What gesture did you choose?

_____

Continue to use this gesture in the future when you notice you are feeling judgmental towards the body you inhabit. Extend compassion and gratitude instead. Notice your breath. Create awareness of all of the things your body is accomplishing with each passing second. Recognize these things as the life-giving gifts that they are.

> *I am fearfully and*
> *wonderfully made;*
> *Wonderful are Your works,*
> *And my soul knows it very well.*
> — Psalm 139:14, King James Bible

Chapter 8: Awakening the Senses[9]

Think of the wonder and awe that babies experience when first learning how to make sense of the world. Sensations are still new, surprising, and joyful experiences. As we grow older, however, we tend to take for granted the amazing gifts of sight, hearing, touch, taste, and smell.

We don't necessarily make the connection between grateful living and our own senses, but as Brother David Steindl-Rast once wrote, "How can I give a full response to this present moment unless I am alert to its message? And how can I be alert unless all my senses are wide awake?"

Each of the five practices in this chapter was created to focus your attention on one of the five senses. Before we begin the specific practices for each sense, reflect for a moment on your awareness of the gifts of the senses in daily life. Can you think of an activity that you find particularly engages your senses — something that makes you aware that you have eyes that can see or a nose that can smell? One person chose "Jumping in Fall Leaves" as being an activity that captivatingly engages four of her five senses. She described the crackling sound of the jumping, the smell of autumn leaves, the texture of the dry leaves underfoot, and the sight of the flaming oranges, browns, and reds.

Name one activity that you find especially awakens your senses.

---

[9] Adapted from: "The Practice of Using Your Nose," formerly on Gratefulness.org

and from "A Good Day," by Brother David Steindl-Rast on Gratefulness.org at http://www.gratefulness.org/resource/a-good-day-audio/

and from "Encounter with God Through The Senses," by Brother David Steindl-Rast on Gratefulness.org at http://www.gratefulness.org/resource/encounter-god-senses/

Name some of the smells, sounds, sights, tastes, or sensations you associate with the activity.

_____

_____

_____

_____

_____

_____

_____

_____

_____

When and to what do your senses respond most readily? If I ask myself this question, I think immediately of working in the garden. The hermitage where I am privileged to live for the better part of each year has a small garden. For fragrance, I grow jasmine, pineapple mint, sage, thyme, and eight different kinds of lavender. What an abundance of delightful smells on so small a patch of ground! And what variety of sounds: spring rain, autumn wind, all year around the birds — mourning dove, blue jay, and wren; the hawk's sharp cry at noon and the owl's hooting at nightfall — the sound the yard-broom makes on gravel, wind chimes, and the creaking garden gate. Who can translate the taste of strawberry or fig into words?

— Brother David Steindl-Rast

Now move on to the following practices, in which you will explore the individual wonders of each of your five senses.

The Sense of Smell[10]

Many people will admit that their sense of smell is sadly underdeveloped. Yet "scent is the most powerful memory trigger," according to the *Psychology Today* article, "The Science of Scent."[11] Treasured memories are a wonderful source of gratefulness. And scent can deepen your emotional experience of events as they occur. If you are serious about becoming fully alive, why not start with your nose?

> *Memories, imagination, old sentiments, and associations are more readily reached through the sense of smell than through any other channel.*
> — Oliver Wendell Holmes

Practice: The Sense of Smell

STOP whatever you are doing and devote your full attention to being still or slowing down. Close your eyes and breathe deeply. Become conscious of your breath breathing itself. Follow a complete inhale-exhale cycle with your full awareness.

LOOK
When your mind has calmed down, remember a favorite smell from your childhood. Children meet the world with great readiness for surprise. That's why we remember smells that surprised us when we were children. Is there any reason why, as grownups, we should not bring to smells the same ready nose?

Savor the memory that goes along with this childhood smell. It may be a fragrance connected with a special place, a delicious food, or a season of the year, or a loved one. Open your eyes and write down this smell. If more than one favorite childhood fragrance comes to mind, write that down, too. If you'd like, draw a picture of your memory in the space below as well.

_____

_____

_____

_____

[10] Adapted from "The Practice of Using Your Nose" formerly on Gratefulness.org

[11] References: "The Science of Scent," Psychology Today, https://www.psychologytoday.com/collections/201205/the-science-scent

Now, prepare to close your eyes again. This time, think of a favorite smell or smells you enjoy in adulthood. It could be the smell of coffee, or of rain; of freshly turned earth in your garden, or of luxurious perfume. Savor your memories of this fragrance. When you open your eyes, write down what aromas came to your mind.

_____

_____

_____

GO

Share a childhood memory of a favorite smell with another person. Ask them about their memories of aromas from childhood. Use your new awareness to help another person engage with his or her sense of smell. You can do this in person, on the phone, or online. Continue to repeat this exercise, whenever you like, as often as you like.

What memories of smells did your conversation bring up? Write down the results of your sharing discussion.

_____

_____

_____

The Ongee of the Andaman Islands don't say, "How are you?" but "Konyuneonorange-tanka?" which means, "How is your nose?" Good manners demand the answer, "I feel heavy with fragrance." We hope you, too, can say this by now!

And may you continue gratefully to enjoy the gift of smells.

The Gift of Sight

Sight is often considered the "primary" sense for human beings, the one which we rely on most for noticing the world around us. Yet, often we take sight for granted, forgetting the wonder of this gift.

Before you begin this exercise, you may wish to go outside, or find a place near a window where you can look out at the larger world. You can, however, do this exercise anywhere. Just grab a pen and this workbook.

> *Begin by opening your eyes, and be surprised that you have eyes you can open. Look at the incredible array of colors that is constantly offered to us for our pure enjoyment.*
> — Brother David Steindl-Rast, "A Good Day"

Practice: Seeing With Open Eyes

STOP whatever you are doing, close your eyes, and focus on your breathing until you feel yourself soften into it. Concentrate on the darkness behind your closed eyelids. Notice that closing your eyes is not really the same as "seeing nothing." Your eyes continue to see; it is simply that the world is blocked from your view.

LOOK

Then, open your eyes. What do you see? Take in as much of the surrounding world as you can. Look up. Look down.

What are three things you can name within your view that are pleasing to your eye? Write them down.

_____

_____

_____

GO

Take a 20-minute walk, and on the way, take three photos of things that make you grateful for the gift of vision. You can use any kind of camera, including your cell-phone camera, to take the snapshots. When you see something that pleases your eyes, take a picture. Try to capture what it is about this thing that makes you appreciate having eyes to see it. Is it a particular part about a view you love, or a particular flower on a plant, an animal, a mural? It doesn't need to be a fancy or "beautiful" thing, just something you are glad you have eyes to see.

In this exercise, the goal is to GO through your walk while LOOKING for beautiful sights. It's fine to take a few more than three snapshots, but try not to get carried away and start taking pictures of everything you see. It's often said that people are far too addicted to taking photos on their cell phones, and consequently fail to notice and appreciate the world around them. At the end of your walk, you will be choosing just three snapshots.

What did you see? If you are able to print out your snapshots, paste them into this book.

If not, simply write down what you chose to photograph.

_____

_____

_____

_____

_____

_____

_____

_____

_____

_____

_____

_____

_____

_____

_____

_____

_____

_____

_____

_____

The Sense of Touch

Touch is truly the most fundamental sensation, though often sight gets the most attention. Touch is so basic that we truly don't notice it most of the time. We notice it most when it's related to touching others — being that it is a profound expression of communication, expressing feelings of affection, comfort, love, friendship, and warmth, as well as sensuality and romantic love. The power of touch is that it is a fundamental source of human connection. In this section, however, we are focused on awakening the senses, so our exercise for touch is focused on the basic sensation of touch itself.

Practice: The Sense of Touch

STOP
Gather together a small array of objects (nothing that can cut you or otherwise harm you when you touch it). Put some thought into making them varied textures: a fuzzy toy, a metal spoon, a rubber ball, a feather, a smooth pebble, a candle, a small sculpture. Gather at least six different objects.

Place the items in a large basket or box, or simply spread the items out on a table.

LOOK
Close your eyes or blindfold yourself. Identify each object by touch with eyes closed. As you touch the objects, be aware of the texture and temperature changes between each: the coldness of metal, the warm feel of fuzzy fabric, the stickiness of wax. Remember the feel of each.

GO
When you open your eyes, write down your impressions.

What objects did you choose? What were some differences between the feel of each object?

_____

_____

_____

_____

_____

_____

The Gift of Hearing

In the womb, we can already hear not only our mother's heartbeat, but even noises from the outside world. The sense of hearing is tied deeply to most of human communication, based as it is around speech. With our ears, we can listen to the songs of birds, or great works of music. What would happen if we decided to not take this remarkable ability for granted?

Practice: Hearing With Open Ears

STOP
For this practice, you can select a favorite recording of music, or choose a place with pleasant ambient sounds, such as a nature area. Plan to keep your eyes closed for three to five minutes while you focus on the sound.

LOOK
Keeping your eyes closed, listen to the sounds around you with your full attention. If you are outside in nature, notice the many small sounds that may increase as you sit in stillness and the creatures around you relax to your presence. Be aware of the buzzing of insects, wind in branches, and the many different songs of birds. If you are listening to music, notice all of the different parts. How many instruments are playing? Can you identify them? What is the highest note you can hear? The lowest note? How do all of the parts interact with one another?

> *How fit to employ all the heart and the soul and the senses forever in joy!*
> — Robert Browning

Allow all of the sounds to swirl around you. Did you know that sound waves are a tangible force, moving through the air? Feel the sensation of the sound as it moves.

GO
When your three to five minute meditation is up, consider what you just experienced. Did you hear anything that you hadn't noticed before in your environment or in the piece of music that you chose? What did you hear?

_____

_____

_____

_____

_____

Imagine some of your favorite sounds. These could be anything: music, a child's laugh, the voice of a loved one, a cat's purr, the sound of rain.

Write down three of your favorite sounds.

_____

_____

_____

_____

_____

_____

Share the gift of sounds with a friend. Listen to a favorite song together, or ask what the sounds are that make your friend enjoy having the gift of hearing. Write your thoughts on this experience.

_____

_____

_____

_____

_____

_____

_____

The Gift of Taste[12]

In addition to cultivating your sense of taste, the following practice, "Raisin Meditation," can promote mindful eating and foster a healthier relationship with food. It is also one of the most basic and widely used methods for cultivating mindfulness in general. In fact, this simple exercise is often used as an introduction to the practice of mindfulness. It requires you to focus your attention on each of your senses as you eat a raisin. Try it with a single raisin — you might find that it's the most delicious raisin you've ever eaten.

Practice: Raisin Meditation

STOP
Find a moment to set aside for this meditation. Make sure you have a raisin before you begin. Take a raisin and hold it in the palm of your hand or between your finger and thumb.

LOOK
Taste is inextricably linked to the sensations of smell and touch. Hold the raisin beneath your nose. With each inhalation, take in the fragrance of the raisin. Now slowly bring the raisin up to your lips, noticing how your hand and arm know exactly how and where to position it. Gently place the raisin in your mouth, without chewing, noticing how it gets into your mouth in the first place. Spend a few moments focusing on the sensations of having it in your mouth, exploring it with your tongue.

When you are ready, prepare to chew the raisin, noticing how and where it needs to be for chewing. Then, very consciously, take one or two bites into it and notice what happens in the aftermath, experiencing any waves of taste that emanate from it as you continue chewing. Without swallowing yet, notice the bare sensations of taste and texture in your mouth and how these may change over time, moment by moment. Also pay attention to any changes in the object itself.

GO
Try applying your newfound sensitivity to taste when you eat your next meal or snack. Can you get through a full meal while remembering to taste each mouthful?

Write down your impressions of this "savoring meal." What did you notice about the sensations of taste as you ate?

_____

_____

_____

[12] Adapted from "Raisin Meditation" from the Greater Good Website http://ggia.berkeley.edu/practice/raisin_meditation

Imagine if your meals consisted only of a small pill that conveniently combined all of your nutrients, but had no taste at all. What would you miss the most if food had no taste?

If food had no taste, I would miss:

_____

_____

_____

If you want to explore the awakening of taste further, keep a journal for a full day, making each meal a savoring meal. Note how your approach to meals changes over the course of one day.

Of course, every meal of your life could be a savoring meal if you give it your full awareness. You can choose to give the sense of taste your full focus whenever you like. And may you continue to enjoy awareness of your sense of taste.

Continue to bring your gratefulness for the gifts of your senses to each day of your life.

> *I am grateful for what I am and have.*
> *My thanksgiving is perpetual.*
> — Henry David Thoreau

PART 2

Strengthening Relationships Through Gratitude

Chapter 9: The Power of Thank You[13]

In his essay, "Gratitude is Contagious," a summer camp director named Richard Bernstein described what happened when he gave kids the opportunity to express thanks. On the first day of camp, he left a "Thank You" jar in front of the dining hall — just a plastic jar, some pencils, and 20 slips of paper, so that campers could leave anonymous expressions of appreciation.

"I figured that would be enough for the rest of the day, maybe the rest of the week," Bernstein recounted. But by lunch that day, he was surprised to see the stack of paper was already gone, and the jar was filling up. Within four hours, forty notes had filled the jar. The notes said thank you for things like sharing a teddy bear, finding a hat, or telling a bedtime story. Bernstein read the notes at evening announcements, and replaced the jar. Soon the jar was receiving almost 200 notes per day.

[13] Adapted from: "Gratitude is Contagious," by Richard Bernstein, formerly on Gratefulness.org

And "Authentic Appreciation," by Terry Pearce, on Gratefulness.org at http://gratefulness.org/resource/authentic-appreciation/

"Why Gratitude Is Good" by Robert Emmons, from the Greater Good Science Center website at http://greatergood.berkeley.edu/article/item/why_gratitude_is_good/

"What is Gratitude," by Robert Emmons, from the Greater Good Science Center website at http://greatergood.berkeley.edu/topic/gratitude/definition

"YES! With Thanks," by Br. David Steindl-Rast, on Gratefulness.org http://gratefulness.org/resource/yes-with-thanks/

"The Art of The Thank You," by Sage Cohen, from the Greater Good Science Center website at http://greatergood.berkeley.edu/article/item/art_thank_you/

Bernstein explained the shift in mood that happened in the camp as the Thank You jar filled up every day. "The camp seemed to take on a different feel. Campers and counselors seemed more conscious of doing things for each other. The process of saying thank you appeared to be generating acts of kindness and consideration." Scientific research backs up Bernstein's perception of gratitude's effect on social relationships in the camp. Along with gratitude's beneficial effects on happiness, health and resiliency, gratitude fundamentally strengthens relationships. As Robert Emmons, one of the leading scientific researchers on gratitude, says: "The social benefits are especially significant here because, after all, gratitude is a social emotion. I see it as a relationship-strengthening emotion because it requires us to see how we've been supported and affirmed by other people."

Studies conducted by Robert Emmons, Michael McCullough, Sonja Lyubomirsky, and many others have shown that gratitude makes us feel closer and more committed to friends and romantic partners, encourages a more equitable division of labor between people, promotes forgiveness, and creates a more compassionate and altruistic environment.

Yet studies also show that authentic expressions of gratitude are relatively rare. In this chapter of the workbook, we'll find more ways to say thank you while noticing the happy results of gratitude expressed.

Thank you!

We all know how to say thank you — or do we? Most of us are trained, as children, to say "Thank you" — but only in certain, specific moments, such as after receiving a birthday gift. There's also a big difference between rote thanks (a simple parroting of the phrase "Thank You") and authentic appreciation. Real gratitude requires us to take the time to pause and truly appreciate what others are doing for us. In the following practice, we relearn the art of the Thank You.

Practice: The Art of The Thank You

STOP

The first step is pausing to make the decision to express gratitude in the first place. In her essay, "The Art of the Thank You," Sage Cohen discusses what happened when she contacted some people to thank them for their excellent work in recent projects. She was saddened to find that they were shocked that she'd called them just to say thanks — usually, they told her, people only called with complaints.

Today, make an effort to notice and feel grateful for something positive someone does for you. This positive thing doesn't need to be out of the ordinary. It could be something this person does every day; the difference is that today you will take the time to notice and appreciate it. Or, it could be a random act by a complete stranger. The important part is that your gratitude is authentic.

LOOK

Take a closer look at what it is you feel grateful for. To give thanks that make the most impact, be specific in your expression of gratitude. "Thank you" is a phrase that is often parroted by rote. So instead of just saying thanks, tell the person what you're thanking them for. By naming what you're thanking the person for, you show you've really noticed their action.

GO

Go for it — tell that person you're grateful! Take careful note of the results of saying thank you. You'll be writing them down in this workbook.

What did you say "Thank You" for today? Who did you thank?

_____

_____

_____

What was it about this person's actions that made you feel most appreciative?

_____

_____

_____

What were the results of saying "Thank You"? Take notes on what you perceive as long-term results, as well as the person's reaction in the short-term.

_____

_____

_____

_____

_____

How did you feel?

_____

_____

_____

_____

_____

Try thanking someone every day for one week. At the end of the week, write down what you think were the main results of this experience.

_____

_____

_____

_____

_____

_____

Chapter 10: What If You Never Met?[14]

It's easy to take the important people in our lives for granted, but research suggests that if we experience and express gratitude for them, our relationships will be stronger and our lives will be happier. This exercise is designed to stoke feelings of gratitude for one of these people — such as a romantic partner or close friend — by asking you to think about what your life might have been like had you never met him or her. By getting a taste of their absence, you should be able to appreciate their presence in your life more deeply — without actually having to lose them for real. When we consider the circumstances that led to a chance encounter, we may be surprised by how unlikely that meeting actually was, and how lucky we were that it happened as it did. Mental subtraction counteracts our tendency to take positive events in our lives — such as meeting a great person — as givens.

> *In normal life we hardly realize how much more we receive than we give, and life cannot be rich without such gratitude. It is so easy to overestimate the importance of our own achievements compared with what we owe to the help of others.* — Dietrich Bonhoeffer

---

[14] Based on a practice from the Greater Good Science Website: http://ggia.berkeley.edu/practice/mental_subtraction_relationships

Practice: Mental Subtraction of Relationships, or "What if You Never Met?"

STOP

Take a moment to think about an important relationship in your life, such as a close friendship, a romantic relationship, a family member, or a teacher.

LOOK

How is your life different because of this person? Think back to where and how you met. Consider the ways in which you might never have met this person and never formed a friendship or relationship — for example, if you hadn't decided to go to a certain party, taken a certain class, or moved to a certain city. When we consider the circumstances that led to a chance encounter, we may be surprised by how unlikely that meeting actually was.

GO

Bring to mind some of the joys and benefits you have enjoyed as a result of this relationship — and consider how you would feel if you were denied all of them. Write down at least two benefits this relationship has brought you. If you feel like adding more than two, go for it! There is no limit.

_____

_____

_____

_____

_____

_____

Write down all of the possible events and decisions — large and small — that could have gone differently and prevented you from meeting this person.

_____

_____

_____

_____

_____

Now, imagine what your life would be like now if events had unfolded differently and you had never met this person. Start from when you first met. Name some things that are better in your life because of this person.

_____

_____

_____

_____

_____

_____

Now that you have considered how things might have turned out differently, appreciate that these benefits were not inevitable in your life. Allow yourself to feel grateful that things happened as they did and this person is now in your life.

Try to make time to perform this practice for several weeks in a row, spending 15 minutes focusing on a different person each week. It might help to do this practice at the same time each week — before bed each Sunday evening, say, or at lunch every Friday.

> *If I had a flower for every time I thought of you, I could walk through my garden forever.* — Alfred Tennyson

Chapter 11: Letter of Thanks[15]

Feeling gratitude can improve health and happiness; expressing gratitude also strengthens relationships. Yet sometimes expressions of thanks can be fleeting and superficial. This exercise encourages you to express gratitude in a thoughtful, deliberate way by writing—and, ideally, delivering—a letter of gratitude to a person you have never properly thanked.

The letter affirms positive things in your life and reminds you how others have cared for you—life seems less bleak and lonely if someone has taken such a supportive interest in us. Visiting the giver allows you to strengthen your connection with her and remember how others value you as an individual.

Steve Farber, a fellow devotee of leadership and a superb public speaker will frequently ask his audience: "How many of you have ever received a note from someone expressing sincere appreciation for something you did?" Most in the audience will raise their hands. "And how many of you still have that note?" Again, most will keep their hands up. He goes on to ask how long the members of the audience have kept the notes. "Five years?" "Ten years?" "Twenty years?" Many hands remain even as Steve asks "Twenty-five years?" But the record is forty years, and when Steve asked his respondent if he remembered what the note said, the person reached into his pants pocket and pulled the note from his wallet. After forty years, he still considered it one of his most prized possessions.

Have you ever kept a similar note? What are your opinions and feelings about the person who wrote it?

_____

_____

---

[15] Adapted from the practice "Write a Letter of Thanks" from the Greater Good In Action website at http://ggia.berkeley.edu/practice/gratitude_letter

and the essay "Authentic Appreciation" by Terry Pearce on Gratefulness.org http://gratefulness.org/resource/authentic-appreciation/

Practice: Letter of Thanks

STOP

Decide you are going to make the effort to write a letter of gratitude. Set aside some private time to write in this journal in the space provided on page 48. You will be working out what you want to say in this workbook, then creating a final draft of your letter of thanks before you give the letter to the person you've chosen. You may want to get some nice stationary ready for the final draft of your letter.

LOOK

Call to mind someone who did something for you for which you are extremely grateful but to whom you never expressed your deep gratitude. This could be a relative, friend, teacher, romantic partner, or colleague. Try to pick someone who is still alive and could meet you face-to-face in the next week. It may be most helpful to select a person or an act that you haven't thought about for a while — something that isn't always on your mind.

> *At times our own light goes out and is rekindled by a spark from another person. Each of us has cause to think with deep gratitude of those who have lighted the flame within us.* — Albert Schweitzer

GO

Now, write a letter to one of these people. You'll need to make a final copy that you can give away when you are done. As you write, remember the following guidelines:

Write as though you are addressing this person directly ("Dear _____"). Don't worry about perfect grammar or spelling. Describe in specific terms what this person did, why you are grateful to this person, and how this person's behavior affected your life.

Try to be as concrete as possible.

Describe what you are doing in your life now and how you often remember his or her efforts.

Try to keep your letter to roughly one page (about 300 words).

Letter of Gratitude

Dear _____

_____

_____

_____

_____

_____

_____

_____

_____

_____

_____

_____

_____

_____

_____

_____

_____

_____

_____

_____

_____

_____

_____

Next, you should try, if at all possible, to deliver your letter in person, following these steps:

Plan a visit with the recipient. Let that person know you'd like to see him or her and that you have something special to share, but don't reveal the exact purpose of the meeting. When you meet, let the person know that you are grateful to him or her and would like to read a letter expressing your gratitude; ask that he or she refrains from interrupting until you're done.

Take your time reading the letter. While you read, pay attention to his or her reaction as well as your own.

After you have read the letter, be receptive to his or her reaction and discuss your feelings together.

Remember to give the letter to the person when you leave.

If physical distance keeps you from making a visit, you may choose to arrange a phone or video chat. Research suggests that while there are benefits to simply writing the letter, you reap significantly greater benefits from delivering and reading it in person. When researchers tested five different exercises, the gratitude visit showed the greatest positive effect on participants' happiness one month later; however, six months after the visit, their happiness had dropped back down to where it was before. This is why some researchers suggest doing this exercise regularly.

Chapter 12: Sympathetic Joy: Social Support for Positive Events[16]

The people close to us need our support when things go right, not just when they go wrong. Providing encouragement for another person's positive event can not only increase the satisfaction they derive from that event, but it can also make them feel loved and cared about. Talking about a positive event together creates a shared positive experience that can enhance overall relationship satisfaction.

During a laboratory-based interaction, romantic partners who responded to each other's news of positive events in the active-constructive style described above reported greater relationship well-being and were less likely to have broken up two months later.

In her essay, *Sympathetic Joy: The Third Abode,* Joan Halifax Roshi talks about the concept of Sympathetic Joy, which is one of the four universal virtues — "Boundless Abodes" — in

> *One of the sanest, surest, and most generous joys of life comes from being happy over the good fortune of others.*
> — Archibald Rutledge

Buddhism. Though feeling and expressing happiness for another's good fortune may seem as if it is something that would happen naturally, in reality this quality is one that

[16] Adapted from the Greater Good in Action exercise "Capitalizing on Positive Events" at http://ggia.berkeley.edu/practice/capitalizing_on_positive_events

and from "Sympathetic Joy: The Third Abode," by Roshi Joan Halifax on Gratefulness.org at http://www.gratefulness.org/resource/sympathetic-joy/

usually needs some deliberate cultivation. As Roshi says: "One of the hardest things for many of us to do is to feel happy when something good happens to another person. Judgment and envy, the tendency to compare and demean, and greed and prejudice narrow our world and make sympathetic joy nearly impossible to experience…

Learning to feel joy for others can help transform our own suffering and self-centeredness into joy."

> *Whatever we intend for another person we experience ourselves, whatever we give we gain, whatever we offer flowers in our own mind.*
>
> — Roger Walsh

In the following practice, you hone your skills at noticing, listening, and responding to another person's positive experience.

Many people, when they first hear about this exercise, worry that when they try to do it, their responses will sound phony or scripted. However, once they start, people report that it feels natural and easy to do.

Practice: Social Support for Positive Events

STOP

Try to make time for this practice at least once per week. You will need a minimum of five minutes each time you do it.

LOOK

Find a friend, family member, colleague, romantic partner, or other acquaintance to tell you about a good thing that happened to him or her today. It does not matter what type of event or how important it was, as long as it was a positive thing that he or she feels comfortable discussing.

GO

As the other person shares, listen and try to respond in an "active-constructive" manner, meaning that you:

- Make good eye contact, showing that you are interested in and engaged in what they have to say.

- Express positive emotion by smiling, or even cheering (if appropriate!).

- Make enthusiastic comments — e.g., "That sounds great," "You must be so excited," or "Your hard work is definitely paying off."

- Ask constructive questions to find out more about the positive aspects of the event. For example, if the person tells you about receiving recognition at work for a project he or she completed, you could ask for more details about the project, of what aspects of the project he or she feels especially proud, and how it felt to receive recognition for it.

- Comment on the positive implications and potential benefits of the event. For example, "I bet this means you have a better chance of getting a promotion this year." One strategy is to pick a specific aspect of the event that resonates with you and begin by commenting on that: "You seem really happy about what your boss said — tell me more." Or, "It must have been satisfying to do so well on something you worked so hard for."

What were the results of this practice? Write down what happened. Include the immediate result, and also any results you may have noticed later on. Congratulations! Continue to awaken joy in yourself and others by using the simple tips from this practice.

_____

_____

_____

_____

_____

_____

_____

_____

_____

_____

_____

_____

_____

_____

_____

_____

_____

_____

_____

_____

Chapter 13: Gratitude and Romantic Love[17]

What does gratefulness have to do with romantic love? Quite a lot, as it turns out. For the past several years, Sara B. Algoe, Ph.D., has been leading a staff of researchers studying this topic. According to Algoe, "What we've discovered in the past several years of studying gratitude in relationships is that gratitude motivates us and it helps us to make gestures that bind us more closely with our romantic partner."

> *When we give cheerfully and accept gratefully, everyone is blessed.*
> — Maya Angelou

Algoe's research began with a study of gratitude in friendships. When she first expanded her research on gratitude to include romantic relationships, many people questioned why. People would ask: "Aren't people in romantic relationships already bound together?" In fact, Algoe points out; studies show that romantic satisfaction

---

[17] Sources: Sara B. Algoe, Ph.D., of the University of North Carolina, Chapel Hill: speech at the 2014 Greater Good Gratitude Summit

Adapted from "Treasure Chest of Life" Practice, by Chuck Roppel, on Gratefulness.org at http://www.gratefulness.org/resource/treasure-chest-practice/

"Want to Satisfy Your Partner? Give them Some Gratitude," by Adam Hoffman, from the Greater Good Science Center Website at http://greatergood.berkeley.edu/article/item/want_to_satisfy_your_partner_give_them_some_gratitude

"A Surprisingly Simple Way to Feel Madly in Love" by Christine Carter, Ph.D., http://greatergood.berkeley.edu/raising_happiness/post/Gratitude_Relationships/

"Is Your Marriage Losing its Luster?" by Christine Carter, Ph.D., from The Greater Good Science Center website at http://greatergood.berkeley.edu/raising_happiness/post/is_your_marriage_losing_its_luster

with one's partner tends to decline over the years. One reason for this is "hedonic adaptation" — the human tendency to emotionally adapt to things which are a constant in our lives — finding these constants less thrilling over time, and taking them for granted.

Gratitude provides a surprising antidote. When we cultivate our feelings of gratitude toward our partner, we do the opposite of taking them for granted. Authentic gratitude requires that we notice the nice things our partner does for us, or the joy they provide us just by being there. When we express this gratitude, we make our partner feel valued and begin a chain reaction of love and affection.

> *Let us be grateful to people who make us happy; they are the charming gardeners who make our souls blossom.*
> — Marcel Proust

In the following practice, we cultivate feelings of gratitude towards our romantic partner.

Practice: Love Notes

STOP

Find a container to hold your Love Notes and put this container in a safe, private place. You can use anything you like for your Love Notes. A humble shoebox works perfectly, as does a large envelope. You can decorate your container over time if you like, or leave it plain. It's what will be inside that's important!

LOOK

Make up your mind to notice, truly notice, when your partner does something nice for you. This need not be a flashy, grand gesture; in fact, this practice is geared

> *Wake at dawn with a winged heart and give thanks for another day of loving.*
> — Kahlil Gibran

toward breaking through your "hedonic adaptation" so that you notice the little things your partner brings to your life each day. It could be as simple as your partner making you coffee in the morning, picking up the kids from school, or curling up next to you while you sleep.

Take a moment to appreciate this action, as if you were experiencing it for the first time. Or, you could take note of a special moment of a small kindness or shared laughter — the kind of small moment that often passes by without any special acknowledgement. Whatever you notice, write a one-line note about it and put it in your special container.

GO

At the end of the week, look through all of your Love Notes. Savor the sensation of appreciation for your partner. What did you write? Copy Week One's gratitude notes in this workbook.

_____

_____

_____

_____

_____

_____

_____

Each week, take all of the notes that have accumulated, and put them in an envelope or group them together with a paper clip or a ribbon.

Now, go on to Week 2. Continue to notice and be grateful for your partner's actions, but this time, when you do notice, thank your partner, as well as writing out a one-line note and adding it to your collection. Make sure that your thanks are authentically felt, and be specific when you thank your partner. How does he or she react? Take notes in this workbook.

_____

_____

_____

_____

_____

At the end of the week, write about any differences you can perceive in the tone of your relationship, or any incidents you believe were a result of this exercise.

_____

_____

_____

_____

_____

The beauty of keeping Love Notes is twofold. It encourages you to be more appreciative towards your partner in the present moment, and it provides you with a collection of positive moments to look through any time you need a boost.

> *While forgiveness heals the heart of old hurts, gratitude opens it to present love. Gratitude bestows many benefits. It dissolves negative feelings: anger and jealousy melt in its embrace, fear and defensiveness shrink. Gratitude deflates the barriers to love.*
> — Roger Walsh, M.D., Ph.D.

You can keep your Love Notes all to yourself, or you can share them with your partner.

Congratulations! You have just deepened your relationship with the practice of gratitude.

How Gratitude Helps Couples Through Hardship[*]

Marriage can be hard, because *life* can be hard. From challenges at work to financial difficulties to raising children, the stresses of everyday life can create tension and conflict within couples

But a study from researchers at the University of Georgia has shown that a little gratitude can protect marriages from the toxic effects of conflict.

Allen Barton, a postdoctoral researcher and lead author of the study, believes that gratitude might have a Teflon-like effect on a marriage. "Gratitude can really help create an environment where negative events . . . simply bounce off and don't have the same negative effect."

While numerous studies have examined the benefits of expressing "thank you" for one's partner, Barton and his team were curious whether perceiving gratitude from one's spouse could protect couples from the damage that challenges, specifically economic ones, can wreak on a marriage.

Their results, published in *Personal Relationships,* showed that spousal gratitude was the most important predictor of marital quality.

---

* Adam Hoffman, *How Gratitude Helps Couples Through Hardship*

Chapter 14: Cultivating Gratitude in Kids and Teens[18]

In the last decade, several studies have been conducted on the effects of gratitude on children and teens. Results show that the benefits that young people get from gratitude are numerous. As with adults, gratitude makes children and teens more resilient, promotes better sleep, reduces anxiety and depression, and increases happiness and optimism. It makes them feel more connected to their community, their families and their schools.

Jeffrey Froh, a pioneering researcher of gratitude in youth, tested out a gratitude curriculum for children ages eight to eleven, the youngest group to be studied thus far. After one week of daily half-hour lessons, these students showed significant increases in grateful thinking and grateful moods. When all the children in the school were given the chance to write thank-you notes to the PTA after a presentation, the students who'd received gratitude lessons wrote eighty percent more notes than kids who didn't receive the lessons, showing that their enhanced gratitude translated into more grateful behavior.

---

[18] Adapted from "Teaching Gratefulness," by Brother David Steindl-Rast on Gratefulness.org at http://gratefulness.org/resource/teaching-gratefulness/

"Grateful Schools, Happy Schools," by Emily Campbell, from the Greater Good Science Center website at http://greatergood.berkeley.edu/article/item/grateful_schools_happy_schools

"7 Ways to Foster Gratitude in Kids," at http://greatergood.berkeley.edu/article/item/seven_ways_to_foster_gratitude_in_kids

Several other studies, some conducted by Froh and some conducted by the Greater Good Science Center, focused on adolescents and teens. The Greater Good Science center found that grateful teens ages fourteen to nineteen are "more satisfied with their lives, use their strengths to better their community, are more engaged in their schoolwork and hobbies, have higher grades, and are less envious, depressed, and materialistic."[19]

Brother David Steindl-Rast, in his essay, "Teaching Gratefulness," points out that helping children appreciate the world around them can be easier than teaching adults. As Brother David says, "Children have a natural ability to marvel. They are little philosophers in this respect, for, as Plato said, all philosophizing starts with wonderment. It is easy to encourage children to look at the world with amazed eyes." The more social aspect of gratitude calls for us to specifically appreciate the things other people do for us. In this aspect, children and teens have less of a tendency towards being grateful. They have yet to experience living as adults, and often simply take for granted all the many things those around them do to take care of them. As Brother David says: "It takes a certain level of alertness to recognize the gift character of any situation, person, or thing. Recognizing isn't even enough. We must acknowledge our interdependence with others before we can genuinely enjoy the give-and-take which sparks gratefulness."

The most important way to cultivate gratefulness in kids is simply to model gratefulness and mindfulness oneself. Kids learn by emulation, so grateful parents make for grateful kids. It can also be helpful to explicitly explain the concept of gratitude towards other people in a way that kids can understand. The children in Froh's study were taught about three types of realizations that encourage gratitude towards others: that someone has intentionally done something to benefit us, that providing this benefit was costly to them, and that the benefit is valuable to us.

---

[19] Greater Good Science Center Website, "7 Ways to Foster Gratitude in Kids" at http://greater-good.berkeley.edu/article/item/seven_ways_to_foster_gratitude_in_kids

Practice: Cultivating Gratitude in Younger Kids

STOP

Take a moment to think about a simple activity that the child in question greatly enjoys. It should be something that requires the involvement and generosity of other people. These could be adults or other children.

LOOK

What are the aspects of the activity that depend on the voluntary, generous actions of another person?

GO

Talk to the child about the various aspects of the activity that were contributed by this other person. Ask the child several questions to encourage the child to recognize the three things described above, starting with basic questions about the activity itself. For instance, the child could enjoy eating pancakes made by his Grandma. You could talk to the child about how pancakes

> *You can look for moments of wonder, multiple moments of wonder, to share with your students — children or adults — so that even the crustiest and most hardened among them suddenly catches on to the fact that whatever there is, is pure gift.*
>
> — Brother David Steindl-Rast

are made, gradually leading the child to realize that Grandma is making the pancakes, and why (for the child). The intent, of course, should not be to make the child feel guilty, but to get him to be aware that things are being done especially for him, things done from love.

You can repeat this practice whenever it's appropriate. When accompanied by other practices that encourage the child's natural sense of wonder, the caring that results is often spectacular.

For more tips on cultivating gratitude in youngsters, you can refer to the Greater Good Science Center's book, *Making Grateful Kids,* which contains 32 concrete, scientifically based strategies for encouraging gratitude in children.

Chapter 15: Gratitude for Parenting[20]

Now that you've spent some time thinking about all of the things people do for their children, it's time to think about the things your own parents did for you.

Some of you may now be thinking, "Perfect, I'd love to think about that!" Others may be filled with a sense of resentment. We are not in any way trying to downplay the trauma of very abusive childhoods — but the majority of us did not have that experience. For the rest of us we may be hanging on to unnecessary amounts of resentment and blame. In their essay, "The Cost of Blaming Parents," three psychologist/researchers discuss the phenomenon, which began with Freudian analysis, of consistently looking for a parental reason for adult mental troubles. They say, "As psychologists and researchers, we think the emphasis on supporting ongoing anger and blame of parents is a problem in today's psychotherapy and in the culture at large." Though the researchers state that "validating feelings and perceptions" and "learning how to shift from self-blame to rightful anger at our parents" can be crucial steps to healing from a difficult childhood, they are troubled by the tendency to stop at this second step, remaining in a state of unresolved anger and blame. In this practice, we ask that you set aside feelings of resentment or blame, and focus on some good things from your childhood.

[20] Sources: "The Cost of Blaming Parents," by Joshua Coleman, Carolyn Pape Cowan and Philip A. Cowan, from the Greater Good Science Center website at http://greatergood.berkeley.edu/article/item/the_cost_of_blaming_parents

Practice: Gratitude for Parenting

STOP whatever you are doing and devote your full attention to being still or slowing down. Become conscious of your breath breathing itself.

LOOK

Think about the amazing amount of work and dedication required for daily parenting. If you are a parent now, or if you work with children, you know how much effort, love, and giving qualities are required for this challenging task. With compassion and appreciation, extend this awareness of the challenges of parenting to your own parents.

GO

Now write a letter of gratitude to a parent. You can write this letter even if the parent in question is no longer living. Use the "Letter of Gratitude" form in Chapter 11 to create a rough draft of your letter.

(If you have a very troubled relationship with your parents to the point that you are not comfortable writing the letter, we just ask that you write down three good things from your childhood instead, in the space below.)

_____

_____

_____

When writing your letter of gratitude for parenting, please remember the following guidelines:
- Write as though you are addressing your parent directly ("Dear _____").
- Don't worry about perfect grammar or spelling.
- Describe in specific terms why you are grateful, and bring up some good memories from your childhood. Let your parent know how you often remember his or her efforts.

Try to keep your letter to roughly one page (about 300 words).

Next, you should try if at all possible to deliver your letter in person, and if possible, follow these steps:
- Plan a visit with your parent. When you meet, let him or her know that you are grateful to him or her and that you would like to read a letter expressing your gratitude. Ask that he or she refrain from interrupting until you're done.
- Take your time reading the letter. While you read, pay attention to his or her reaction as well as your own.
- After you have read the letter, be receptive to his or her reaction and discuss your feelings together.
- Remember to give the letter to your parent when you leave.

If physical distance prevents you from making a visit, you may choose to arrange a phone or video (Skype) chat. Research suggests that while there are benefits of simply writing the letter, you reap significantly greater benefits from delivering and reading it in person.

Chapter 16: Cultivating Gratitude in The Workplace[21]

According to a survey of 2,000 Americans conducted by the John Templeton Foundation, people are less likely to feel or express gratitude at work than anyplace else.

It's not that people don't crave gratitude at work. Most reported that hearing "thank you" at work made them feel good and motivated. And almost all respondents reported that saying "thank you" to colleagues "makes me feel happier and more fulfilled" — but on a given day, only ten percent acted on that impulse. A stunning 60 percent said they "either never express gratitude at work or do so perhaps once a year."

What's the problem? One reason is the fundamental nature of work itself — a monetary exchange for services rendered, which in many people's minds means that thanks are not needed. Yet people don't just work for money. We also work for respect, for a sense of accomplishment, for a feeling of purpose. We invest our selves and our emotions into our jobs, and work affects our emotional states.

Another reason for the lack of thanks at work is that people fear saying "thank you" will make them vulnerable. Yet, in the Templeton survey, ninety-three percent

[21] Adapted from the essay "Five Ways to Cultivate Gratitude at Work," by Jeremy Adam Smith, from the Greater Good in Action Website at http://greatergood.berkeley.edu/article/item/five_ways_to_cultivate_gratitude_at_work

agreed that grateful bosses are more likely to succeed, and only 18 percent thought that gratitude made bosses "weak." Cultivating a culture of gratitude might be the best way to help a workplace prepare for stresses that come with change, conflict, and failure. Making gratitude a policy and a practice "builds up a sort of psychological immune system that can cushion us when we fall," according to gratitude researcher Robert Emmons. "There is scientific evidence that grateful people are more resilient to stress, whether minor everyday hassles or major personal upheavals."

> *As we express our gratitude, we must never forget that the highest appreciation is not to utter words but to live by them.*
> — John F. Kennedy

Gratitude helps employees to see beyond one disaster and recognize their gains. Ideally, it gives them a tool "to transform an obstacle into an opportunity," as Emmons writes, and reframe a loss as a potential gain.

Building a culture of gratitude at work is not easy, but the science says it's worth it. We need to overcome our aversion to gratitude on the job, and come to see it as just one more career skill we can cultivate alongside skills like communication, negotiation, and forgiveness. It's something anyone can learn — from which everyone will benefit.

The following exercise will help you foster gratitude on the job.

> *Gratitude can transform common days into thanksgivings, turn routine jobs into joy, and change ordinary opportunities into blessings.*
>
> — William Arthur Ward

Practice: Thanks at Work

STOP

Take the time to think about the benefits that saying thanks at work can bring, and then picture the positive effect gratitude can have on your workplace.

LOOK

At any workplace, there are many power imbalances. Gratitude needs to come from the bosses as well as others in the workplace, so if you are a boss, you can really get things started by expressing your appreciation for your employees. Make sure that your thanks are authentic and specific. And make sure that you don't neglect thanking the people who never get thanked. In every workplace there are jobs that tend to be less "in the limelight." Make an effort to notice these daily jobs that keep the company running. Thank the person who brews the coffee in the morning, the mailroom clerk, the people who clean the office, and so on.

What jobs at your workplace do you think go most unnoticed?

_____

_____

_____

_____

_____

GO

Create a "Thanks Box" at work — a box with pens and small slips of paper stacked next to it and a slot on top for dropping in grateful notes. Depending on the atmosphere in your workplace, you may want to make this a space for anonymous notes of thanks, so that people feel more comfortable leaving them.

Check the "Thanks Box" every day, and notice the effect on workplace morale as the thanks in the box continue to grow. You can also go a little further and make a more public display of thanks at your workplace, if you feel it will be received well. You could hang a bulletin board on the wall at work, or create a website where people can post appreciative notes. This way, the thanks can remain visible, creating further feelings of well-being.

In the space below, write down the contents of two of the thank-you notes from the first week of your Thanks Box.

_____

_____

_____

_____

_____

_____

What differences did you notice in office morale from keeping a Thanks Box?

_____

_____

_____

_____

_____

_____

What differences did you notice in your own feelings toward your work and co-workers?

_____

_____

_____

_____

_____

PART 3

Guidance Through the Labyrinth: Gratefulness in Times of Trouble

Chapter 17: Step Back, Step Up, Step Out: Finding Distance From Our Troubles[22]

There are times when every person practicing grateful living asks him or herself:

How can I be grateful if I've got nothing but trouble?

This question pushes through to the very core of gratefulness. Let us begin by frankly admitting that we cannot be grateful for injury, disease, injustice, loss of a loved one, or other such troubles. Certainly, in the midst of many troubles, you may not feel grateful. Even with a grateful attitude toward life, we may or may not feel grateful at certain times. But that doesn't mean we can't still intentionally cultivate an attitude of gratefulness.

When many troubles are weighing on your mind, making fine distinctions between attitude and feelings may not be at the top of your list. Still, you might want to think this through. It will at least take your mind off your problems for a moment, and it might do a lot more for you.

---

[22] Based on several Q & A's with Brother David formerly on Gratefulness.org

We cannot be grateful for all that a given moment brings us; yet, in any given moment, we can be grateful for something — for the opportunity it brings us. Opportunity for what? Only in that particular moment can you hear an answer to this question that will fit your particular need. And you will hear it, if you keep your mind attuned through gratefulness.

Our troubles create a great deal of noise. In the midst of that din, it is not easy to hear the soft voice of opportunity. We need trained ears. This is why we need to train our ears long before trouble breaks in on us.

What is gratefulness like, at those times when your feelings do agree with your attitude? You feel a trust in life that overcomes fear. This trust makes your heart feel wide open and free, the very opposite of those anxious feelings that make you clam up, feelings that squeeze your chest together until you can hardly breathe. When being grateful and feeling grateful are in harmony, it takes a lot to make you feel fatigued; your courageous trust invigorates your body, your mind, and your spirit.

> *Have courage for the great sorrows of life, and patience for the small ones.*
> — Victor Hugo

Now, that deep trust in life is not a feeling but a stance that you deliberately take. It is the attitude we call courage and courage is quite compatible with feeling afraid. In fact, courage presupposes fear; it is the attitude of one who goes ahead in spite of fear, anxiety, and fatigue. And isn't this what you are doing, difficult though it is?

In the following practice, we will explore a modification to the STOP-LOOK-GO technique we've been using in the previous chapters.

Practice: Step Back, Step Up, Step Out!

STEP BACK

Get some distance from whatever causes your stress. We must be grateful that our inner eye has an adjustable lens. Stress within a relationship, stress from world events, stress of any kind — it all slackens somewhat as soon as we shift our focus from close-up to a greater distance. Immediately our field of vision widens and we realize: there is more to life than what makes us so tense. Just sitting still for a while, breathing deeply, is the form this first step often takes.

> *Drag your thoughts away from your troubles... by the ears, by the heels, or any other way you can manage it.*
> — Mark Twain

STEP UP

Rise to a higher level. By doing so we show ourselves grateful for what we may call "our invisible wings." By "stepping up" with courage we can rise above our tension to a great calm. Maybe we should call this not a step but a wing-beat: in trust we spread our wings and soar.

STEP OUT!

Do something for someone or do something creative: in other words, take action! Action can make tension snap. It is a way of showing gratefulness for our innate creativity. Yet, only when it springs from the inner distance and calm of steps one and two will action be truly creative. A sense of tension tends to paralyze us. We must guard against the temptation to break the tension by merely lashing out in some habitual reaction. It takes discipline to wait and to respond only when we are grounded in a quiet center. By waiting, we increase the chance that our response will be a creative step out of tension.

> *Out of suffering have emerged the strongest souls; the most massive characters are seared with scars.*
> — Kahlil Gibran

What we said in the very first chapter of this book about the three steps of being awake, aware, and alert is true also of stepping back, stepping up, and stepping out: these steps are simple, but they are not easy; they take practice. Times of tension challenge us to practice these steps. This can make us grateful. After all, every challenge is an opportunity to go beyond what we knew we could do — an opportunity to grow.

> *Although the world is full of suffering, it is full also of the overcoming of it.*
> — Helen Keller

Times that challenge us physically, emotionally, and spiritually may make it almost impossible for us to feel grateful. Yet, we can decide to live gratefully, courageously open to life in all its fullness. By living the gratefulness we don't feel, we begin to feel the gratefulness we live. This is not a quick and easy recipe, but you will find that it works.

> *When you have hope you actually create a memory of the future that your mind starts working toward.*
> — Marsha Huber

Chapter 18: Inner Peace Through Gratefulness[23]

> *Listening closely, we can hear how similar they sound, the words blessing and blood. Blessing, rightly understood, is the invisible bloodstream pulsating through the universe — alive and life giving. "Just to live is holy," say sthe great Jewish sage Abraham Joshua Heschel. "Just to be is a blessing.*
>
> — Brother David Steindl-Rast

Our inner peace begins with counting our blessings, and fans out to include even the hardest challenges, those that we used to consider a curse. Let's start by looking at the good in our lives. Step by step, we can expand the picture to see how acceptance grows until all of your life is bathed in peace.

---

[23] Based on a practice formerly on Gratefulness.org

Practice: Inner Peace

STOP
Are you really present here and now? Breathe deeply, and sink into this moment. What are you thankful for? (Give yourself a few moments to reflect on this question.)

LOOK
Is there something you are not thankful for? What is it? Spell it out to yourself. Now, write it out below.

_____

_____

_____

Is it really in this present moment? If it's in the past (a painful memory), let go: You want to be present here and now. If it's in the future (an anxiety or fear), let go: You want to be present here and now. If there is something in the present that you can't be thankful for — pain, grief, and confusion — accept it as a given. What is, is. You are confronted with a given reality. You may not be able to be thankful for it, but you can obviously live with it: you are living with it! — at least in this one moment — and that's all you've got. Embrace this truth, not only with your intellect, which is too narrow, but with your whole heart. Let this experience sink in. Do you feel peace, a tiny bit at least?

GO
You can fan this little spark of peace to make it glow a bit brighter. This moment is part of the rhythm of time.

When we are listening to peaceful chanting, or when the sound of bells makes our hearts fly up like a flock of doves from a steeple, it is easy to be present with the given moment, grateful and at peace. A moment later, however, our thoughts surge back to past and future. It is already a step forward in learning inner peace when we notice every time we slip out of the present. What is it that makes you most frequently lose your peace? Face it firmly. Name it clearly. This is an important step: Just to name what makes you lose your peace helps you regain it.

You are not alone. Others are struggling bravely in their attempt to sustain inner peace. You can in turn encourage those who are also seeking peace. And don't forget to keep encouraging yourself. For instance, you can write the word "Now" on a piece of paper and put it where it will catch your eye. You may have your own

> *At any moment the fully present mind can shatter time and burst into Now.*
> — Brother David Steindl-Rast

creative ideas of how to bring your attention back to the present, so that you can hear the message of peace inherent in each moment.

Congratulations! What you can take away with you from this practice is the anchor you have found. Hold on to its chain. You will be able to pull yourself back to inner peace, the peace of being gratefully present in the Now.

A Challenging Past Can Lead to A Happier Present*

A recent study suggests that experiencing adversity can not only equip us to deal with negative events, but also help us appreciate the positive ones, possibly increasing our overall satisfaction with life.

In the study, published in *Psychological Science,* Alyssa Croft of the University of British Columbia and her colleagues surveyed 15,000 adults, asking them to indicate whether they had ever experienced major traumas in the past or were experiencing them in the present; the participants cited discrimination, divorce, death of a spouse, illness or injury, and military combat, among other challenges. The research team also measured the participants' capacities for savoring — that is, how much they prolong and deepen their positive emotional response to pleasurable moments, such as a physical comfort or being in nature.

Although people who were currently struggling with adversity reported a diminished proclivity for savoring positive events, individuals who had dealt with more adversity in the past reported an elevated capacity for savoring. Thus, the worst experiences in life may come with an eventual upside, by promoting the ability to appreciate life's small pleasures.

---

* From "How a Challenging Past Can Lead to a Happier Present," by Linda Graham, for the Greater Good Science Center, and "From Tribulations to Appreciation: Experiencing Adversity in the Past Predicts Greater Savoring in the Present," study by Alyssa Croft, Elizabeth W. Dunn, Jordi Quoidbach.

Chapter 19: Guidance Through the Labyrinth: Navigating through Confusion[24]

> *At some point we all look up and realize we are lost in a maze.*
> — John Green

In times of confusion, the ancient practice of walking a labyrinth takes on a meaning beyond that of its soothing, meditational qualities. It becomes a strong metaphor for finding our way through the maze of decisions we must make. Though the exit from the maze is not visible, it does exist. By continuing our progress forward, we will eventually make it through.

In this practice, we will continue the STOP, LOOK, GO framework we've used in most of this book.

---

[24] Based on a practice formerly on Gratefulness.org

Practice: Navigating through Confusion

STOP

Entering an authentic feeling is something we'd rather avoid. We tend to rush around and take on more and more activities so that we don't have time to look too closely at feelings we fear may make us uncomfortable. We must stop this movement and turn it around so that we can quiet down enough to see our way through whatever is bothering us.

> *It is an ironic habit of human beings to run faster when they have lost their way.*
> — Rollo May

If you haven't done so already, take a moment now to focus on a particular concern for which you'd like guidance. This could be a blurred area in a relationship, a life choice you need to make, a darkness into which you want to let light flow, or a quality you wish you could develop in yourself. The image of a tree reflected on a pond gets blurred when wind agitates the water. You need to wait and let the surface of your mind calm down in order to see clearly.

LOOK

Below, write down in the briefest form the gist of your concern. It sometimes is a good idea to draw a little image or series of pictographs like early people drew on the walls of caves. Sometimes these image-scribbles are closer to our souls than written words, just as mythic stories are closer to our hearts than factual accounts. At the end, draw a door or write the word "entrance."

Recall how you feel when you are about to enter a door for an important visit and you rehearse once more what you want to say. Formulate your concern, as if you were going to tell it to a friend. Now you are entering the labyrinth, which, like a friend, will listen, and so allow clarity to emerge deep in your heart.

Now you will practice the discipline of walking the labyrinth. With a pencil, trace the path through the labyrinth below. When you get to the center, pause for a while and hold your concern quietly in your heart.

Now, make your way back through the labyrinth. As you find your way out, visualize your tension and confusion lightening with each turn you make. When you reach the entrance again, picture your worry being left behind.

Congratulations! You didn't get sidetracked, or if you did, you made your meanderings part of the process.

By going through this practice, you have shared in a ritual that people have performed for centuries. Think of the thousands of others who have walked this path before you. Like you, they have found that the mere process of walking step by step, wing-beat by wing-beat, brings of itself greater clarity in daily life.

> The most beautiful people we have known are those who have known defeat, known suffering, known struggle, known loss, and have found their way out of the depths. These persons have an appreciation, a sensitivity, and an understanding of life that fills them with compassion, gentleness, and a deep loving concern.
>
> — Elisabeth Kübler-Ross

Think of others who are in the midst of confusion and inner turmoil and send them your compassionate good wishes. And may you feel greater peace as you navigate the twists and turns of life.

Chapter 20: Healing the Mind[25]

Abundant research has shown that mental health is every bit as vital to well-being as physical health, and yet our emotional struggles can make us feel isolated and/or ashamed. These "secondary" feelings only compound our challenges. Our longings for contentment and happiness can feel overwhelming, especially if we have no road map. Yet, in so many ways, we have far more agency than we know or use.

Emotions and thoughts come and go like the weather. In the midst of life, we experience feelings on the spectrum from desirable to undesirable, and from easy to challenging, most every day. Grateful living can help us reorient our mind to become more accepting, compassionate, and curious about our thoughts and feelings. And we can work with habits of the mind, as opposed to against them: learning with awareness from all of our moment-to-moment thoughts and feelings. Cultivating gratitude can bring about this sort of shift in perspective.

Some of us experience a level of depression that is all-pervasive. Brother David recalls a letter from a man who described being "engulfed in a blackness that makes gratefulness seemingly futile." This level of depression can be situational (for instance, when one is grieving), or it can be a mood disorder that isn't based on outward

---

[25] Adapted from "Healing the Mind," on Gratefulness.org at http://www.gratefulness.org/area-of-interest/healing-the-mind/

circumstances. Seeking professional treatment is crucial if you have this kind of mood disorder, whether or not you decide to medicate. There are also other things you can do to help, including the practice at the end of this chapter. Meditation has been shown to improve bleak mental states. Also, many studies have shown that regular exercise is a big help in lessening the symptoms of depression. Brother David, who also suffers from depressive periods, advises regular walks, along with some other practical tips that can help during these times.

"I'll be glad to share with you what helps me (a little) when depressions come over me:

- *to go for walks (even if I don't feel like it);*
- *to stick with my regular schedule;*
- *not to force feelings of gratefulness (it won't work);*
- *to remind myself that "this, too, will pass";*
- *to treat myself kindly, as I would treat a suffering friend;*
- *to do something — no matter how small — for someone else (merely a smile, or a kind greeting will help loosen the prison bars of depression)."*

— Brother David Steindl-Rast

Now, please dive into the following practice, which will help you explore (and thus help you combat) your most troubled moods.

Practice: Awareness of, and Compassion for, your Troubling Moods

STOP whatever you are doing and devote your full attention to being still or slowing down. If it helps, close your eyes. Become conscious of your breath breathing itself. Follow one complete inhale-exhale cycle with your attention.

Bring your awareness to the present moment, and allow yourself to sink into it. Put your hand on your heart. See if you can focus on your breath while letting your heart soften.

LOOK

We are liberated by being able to identify the nuances of our feelings. All feelings are gifts reminding us that we are still fully alive — on the inside. There is good news in the fact that we can feel at all. It is really good news that we are tender-hearted and capable of feeling — even things that we might not like to feel. It means we are human. And being human is a big, vulnerable job.

Allow your attention to turn towards how you are feeling right now. The first thing that often happens is we have a story that immediately wants to explain our feelings and that wants a lot of attention. Underneath that story are important feelings. Can you get past the story to at least one feeling, clearly? Does it arise with a name? Try naming the feeling softly to yourself.

Challenging feelings are what connect us to the rest of the human race, and often, ironically, what make us most lovable. As Leonard Cohen says: "Ring the bells that still can ring. Forget your perfect offering. There is a crack in everything. That's how the light gets in."

GO

Develop a posture of grateful kindness towards yourself, as you might extend yourself to someone else. Notice that you can be compassionate toward your emotions and that compassion can change the quality of how you feel about your feelings.

> *Like a ship in dense fog, you will have to go on automatic pilot. But the fog will lift. Better still, your going forward gets you out of the fog. As you stay open in grateful trust, grateful feelings will start to bud.*
>
> — Brother David

Remember times when you have had challenging feelings in your past — and notice that they could shift, sometimes completely. Connect with the impermanence of feelings — like the weather, they change and move like clouds through the sky of our lives.

Write about the nuances, physical sensations, and/or "the weather" of your feelings below. You can learn a lot by letting yourself excavate and name small feelings under the bigger ones. You can draw a picture if you prefer. What did you unearth when you allowed yourself to listen to your emotions?

_____

_____

_____

_____

_____

Now, notice how your compassion for yourself can translate into greater compassion for others. There is a wonderful quote: "Be kinder than necessary, for everyone you meet is fighting some kind of battle." Extend yourself with care to someone in need today.

Act with generosity toward someone. Direct your attention toward a hurt you might be able to help heal. It is amazing how easy it is to "make someone's day" with an act of kindness, and it is remarkable how much focusing on helping others can ripple back to helping us feel better about life.

Chapter 21: Trusting Life: Facing Your Fears[26]

The modern world is often an anxious place, as Rollo May points out in his book, *The Age of Anxiety*. The lack of a solid "set of rules" to follow is freeing, but it can also cause we human beings to feel ungrounded and hollow. In such a space, it is common to be beset by a generalized feeling of anxiety, which can lead to a flurry of unreasonable fears. If you feel you are beset by such fears, this next practice can be very helpful.

> *Can you feel grateful for not knowing what will come next? Gratefulness is a way of dealing with your fear of not-knowing. Whenever you get a package and you say, "Thank you," you have expressed your trust in the giver, not your appreciation of the gift. You haven't even looked yet at what's inside. If you wait to look first at what's inside, and then you decide whether or not to say, "Thank you," you will not be considered a particularly grateful person. By making peace with "not-knowing," you can eliminate much of the fear that troubles your mind.*
>
> — Brother David Steindl-Rast

---

[26] Adapted from "Trusting Life," by Brother David Steindl-Rast, on Gratefulness.org at http://www.gratefulness.org/resource/trusting-life/

Practice: Facing Unreasonable Fears

STOP

Living with unreasonable fears is a burden that is not necessary or healthy. It takes effort, however, to gain freedom from that burden. To do so, you must make the decision to undertake a task for which you will naturally feel aversion — identifying and facing your unreasonable fears. It always takes courage to face fears, even unreasonable ones — sometimes *especially* unreasonable ones! So the first step is to decide to bravely stop what you are doing and look at your fears.

Find a comfortable place, and focus on your breathing until you feel calm and peaceful. Devote your full attention to being still or slowing down. If it helps, close your eyes. Become conscious of your breath breathing itself. Follow one complete inhale-exhale cycle with your attention.

> *You gain strength, courage, and confidence by every experience in which you really stop to look fear in the face. You must do the thing which you think you cannot do.*
> — Eleanor Roosevelt

Bring your awareness to the present moment, and allow yourself to soften into it. No matter where you are, make an effort to tune into the vastness around you. Picture yourself somewhere with the ability to see far and wide around you. Be at peace and feel compassion for what you feel.

LOOK

To tackle your unreasonable fears, you must first identify them. Some people have an irrationally excessive fear reaction to things like spiders, or heights, or the sight of blood, or deep water. These are all things that many people are uncomfortable with, but an unreasonable amount of fear reaction towards a particular thing can limit your happiness and the breadth of your experiences. Only you can determine which fears are problematic for you. For some people, the fear of potential embarrassment is their biggest setback, leading to a phobic reaction to things like public speaking, or even of taking small chances like offering their opinion at work or trying something they've never tried before.

Make a little list of your fears in the space below. Name as many as you can think of. Don't try to differentiate between reasonable and unreasonable fears — just write down anything that comes to your mind as something that makes you fearful.

_____

_____

_____

_____

_____

Now, take a good look at the list, and circle the ones that you feel are unreasonable. If you're in doubt, give yourself the benefit of the doubt, and say it's a reasonable fear. There will be plenty of unreasonable ones left. Then, among those unreasonable ones, pick the one that you think you can deal with, very much like when you were a child afraid of the dark. Perhaps some time when it was already dark, your father sent you out to the garden to pick up something that you forgot out there. You rushed out, and you

> *Avoiding danger is no safer in the long run than outright exposure. The fearful are caught as often as the bold.*
> — Helen Keller

were whistling to yourself and encouraging yourself as best you could. Then you came back and saw that nothing had happened. That made you stronger and helped you overcome the fear. By overcoming one particular fear, you became more courageous altogether.

GO

Begin by choosing one fear to deal with, and resolve to tackle that fear by doing. We will not promise you, though, that nothing will happen to you when you do what you fear. No! Sometimes what happens to us is much worse than we could possibly have anticipated. But in the end we discover that we come out more alive than before, if we brave it. If we don't brave it, we run around with that fear. And that diminishes our lives.

Choose one of those unreasonable fears that you can just barely handle. In that little area, do what you're most afraid of, and see what happens. Just as our courage is of one piece, so our fear is of one piece. All those different fears that we could name are of one piece. So if we tackle the weakest one, the one with which we can just barely deal, we have tackled the whole bunch of them.

What fear did you choose to face? What were the results? Write, draw, or collage your experience into this workbook.

_____

_____

_____

_____

_____

Congratulations! You have dwelt on a subject that most people go out of their way to avoid — your fears. In doing so, you have shown great courage. Acknowledge the strength and character within yourself, which you have manifested by going through with this exercise. And go forth into the world a little more alive and awake.

Chapter 22: Reframing Disaster: Finding the Value in Negative Past Experiences[27]

If you are troubled by a past unpleasant experience, you might consider trying to reframe how you think about it using the language of thankfulness.

Let us be clear: to say that gratitude is a helpful strategy to handle hurt feelings does not mean that we should try to ignore or deny suffering and pain. To deny that life has its share of disappointments, frustrations, losses, hurts, setbacks, and sadness would be unrealistic and untenable.

Processing a life experience through a grateful lens does not mean denying negativity. It is not a form of superficial happyology. Instead, it means realizing the power you have to transform an obstacle into an opportunity. It means reframing a loss into a potential gain, recasting negativity into positive channels for gratitude.

As the German theologian and Lutheran pastor Dietrich Bonhoeffer once said, "Gratitude changes the pangs of memory into a tranquil joy." We know that gratitude enhances happiness, but why? Gratitude maximizes happiness in multiple ways, and one reason is that it helps us reframe memories of unpleasant events in a way that decreases their unpleasant emotional impact. This implies that grateful coping entails looking for positive consequences of negative events. For example, grateful coping might involve seeing how a stressful event has shaped who we are today and has prompted us to reevaluate what is really important in life.

---

[27] Based on an essay by Robert Emmons "How Gratitude Can Help You Through Hard Times", from the Greater Good Science Center Website at http://greatergood.berkeley.edu/article/item/how_gratitude_can_help_you_through_hard_times

Practice: Reframing Negative Events

STOP

Set aside some time to work on "reframing" a painful event from your past. Recall and report on an unpleasant open memory — a loss, a betrayal, victimization, or some other personally upsetting experience.

LOOK

Now, focus on the positive aspects of a difficult experience — and discover what about it might now make you feel grateful. Do not attempt to deny the negative aspects of the experience, nor ignore the pain. Simply add whatever "silver lining" you can find to the "cloud" of this painful memory.

GO

Write out your answers to the following questions:

What lesson, or lessons, did the experience teach me?

_____

_____

_____

_____

_____

Can I find ways to be thankful for what happened to me now, even though I was not at the time it happened? What ability did the experience draw out of me that surprised me?

_____

_____

_____

_____

_____

Have my negative feelings about the experience limited or prevented my ability to feel gratitude in the time since it occurred?

_____

_____

_____

_____

_____

Has the experience removed a personal obstacle that previously prevented me from feeling grateful? How am I now more the person I want to be because of it?

_____

_____

_____

_____

_____

Remember, your goal is not to relive the experience but rather to get a new perspective on it. Simply rehearsing an upsetting event makes us feel worse about it. However, studies show that those who write about an event and specifically work to see ways it might be redeemed with gratitude gain great benefits. In a study conducted at Eastern Washington University, participants who "reframed" a past event by answering the above questions demonstrated fewer intrusive memories later on, such as wondering why it happened, whether it could have been prevented, or believing they caused it to happen. Thinking gratefully, this study showed, can help heal troubling memories and in a sense redeem them—a result echoed in many other studies. By looking at painful experiences from our past through the lens of gratitude, we can create a sense of healing and satisfaction that we carry forth into the future.

> *Suffering has been stronger than all other teaching . . . I have been bent and broken, but I hope into a better shape.*
> — Charles Dickens

What Doesn't Kill You Makes You Kinder[*]

Researchers at Northeastern University recently conducted a study that shows that living through difficult setbacks may have an unexpected benefit: compassion. The study found that people who had experienced more severe adversity are more empathetic and have a higher likelihood of taking action to relieve the suffering of others.

In one test, a confederate of the researchers posed as a participant who wasn't feeling well. The test subjects who had experienced more adversity were more likely to help the "unwell participant" than the subjects who had experienced less adversity.

---

[*] Jill Suttie, Psy.D., "What Doesn't Kill You Makes You Kinder," for the Greater Good Science Center. Study cited: "Suffering and Compassion: The Links Among Adverse Life Experiences, Empathy, Compassion, and Prosocial Behavior," by Daniel Lim and David DeSteno, published in *Emotion,* 2016.

_____

_____

_____

_____

_____

_____

_____

_____

_____

Chapter 23: Grief and Gratefulness[28]

There is no rulebook for grieving. The varieties of grief are as unique as each rare human being, and it is important to honor the way in which your own grief arises, fluctuates, and runs its course...or even lingers beyond the time you'd expect. Although we have centuries of human experience from which we can see that grief goes through stages, as Dr. Elisabeth Kübler-Ross pointed out — denial, anger, bargaining, depression, and finally, acceptance — these are not stages like chapters in a book where one ends and the next begins. Rather, they tend to weave in and out of each other, so that you might have what seems like a reasonably "good" day one day and then, the next, you are once again overcome with missing your child, your mother, or even everyone and everything you have ever lost in your life.

Can grief prevent you from leading a productive life? Maybe sometimes. In this exercise, we practice processing grief with the help of grateful living.

---

[28] Adapted from a grief practice, formerly on the Gratefulness.org

Adapted from "Lingering Grief," by Patricia Carlson, on Gratefulness.org http://www.gratefulness.org/resource/lingering-grief/,

and from "Gratitude and Grief," by Elaine Mansfield on Gratefulness.org http://www.gratefulness.org/resource/gratitude-and-grief/

Practice: Grief and Gratefulness

STOP

Devote your full attention to being still or slowing down. If it helps, close your eyes. Become conscious of your breath breathing itself. Follow one complete inhale-exhale cycle with your attention. Bring your awareness to the present moment, and allow yourself to soften into it. No matter where you are, make an effort to tune into the vastness around you. Picture yourself somewhere with the ability to see far and wide, into the stars that glitter the cosmos, the expanse of time, and the millions of beings that dwell on this planet.

LOOK

When we're struck by grief, is the main point to "beat" this mood that seems to be clogging the works? There's also healing in giving expression to your grief. It may be a key to finding further depths of feeling about your losses that you still hadn't fathomed. Finding those layers, and writing about them or sharing them with a friend, might make a difference in allowing you to move out of being stuck.

Just as your writing is redeeming, so is art when it depicts grief without prettifying it. The grief of a mother who lived through two world wars erupts in the images of Käthe Kollwitz in a way that touches the heart of all grief. We suggest that you find her paintings at the library or on the internet, and meditate on this icon of human suffering.

> *You will not 'get over' the loss of a loved one; you will learn to live with it. You will heal and you will rebuild yourself around the loss you have suffered. You will be whole again but you will never be the same. Nor should you be the same nor would you want to.*
> — Elizabeth Kübler-Ross

The poet Rilke encourages us to put our trust in the healing power of transformation. He asks, "From what experience have you suffered most?" This, Rilke tells us, will be the experience that has most transformed you.

If you feel able to do so, explore the bitter emotion you are struggling with. Even if an experience crushes you, can it not serve as a wine press that releases an unexpected sweetness? Is there some way in which it allows you to reclaim a part of yourself that you'd forgotten? Did it release

> *The deeper that sorrow carves into your being, the more joy you can contain. Is not the cup that holds your wine the very cup that was burned in the potter's oven? And is not the lute that soothes your spirit, the very wood that was hollowed with knives? When you are joyous, look deep into your heart and you shall find it is only that which has given you sorrow that is giving you joy. When you are sorrowful look again in your heart, and you shall see in truth that you are weeping for that which has been your delight.*
> — Kahlil Gibran

courage, compassion, or a deeper awareness of what matters? Ponder each of these qualities and see if you can find them in your own experience: courage, compassion (for whom?), or a deeper awareness (of what?).

And can you name other sweetnesses that can flow out of the grief that crushes you? Pay attention to the faintest taste of sweetness.

_____

_____

_____

GO

Often what makes grief so bitter is being alone with it. But remember that grief as well as joy is a feeling all of us can share. Sharing doubles our joy and cuts our grief in half. A friend who sits with you, holds your hand, and listens is a great gift.

Support while grieving does not take away grief, but it does allow you to feel less alone with it. Hospice programs often offer grief groups and/or counseling for survivors, and it might be worth checking — if you haven't already — whether you have such services locally. These services are not unique to hospice programs and can also be found by contacting the counseling office of the university nearest you and asking for referrals.

You can also find support over the internet. Computers need not be cold when they serve heart-to-heart contact. You can find forums and message boards to connect with others who are feeling grief. The grief of others puts our own in perspective and helps us not feel so alone in our struggle. In connecting with others, you will be helping them just as they help you — and helping others is another known way to ease your own unhappiness.

Helping others in general (not just those who are grieving) has healing power, taking us from mere preoccupation with ourselves to a more inclusive concern for the sufferings of others. In helping them to heal, we ourselves find healing.

> *I think if you have lost a great happiness and try to recall it, you are only asking for sorrow, but if you do not try to dwell on the happiness, sometimes you find it dwelling in your heart and body, silent but sustaining.*
>
> — Ursula K. Le Guin

You may find in your neighborhood someone who needs a listening ear or helping hand. People farther away — victims of natural catastrophes, injustice, and violence — may seem harder to help, but keep in mind the many organizations like Habitat for Humanity and Amnesty International that give you avenues for reaching out.

Whatever you chose and whatever you continue to choose to do, know that you are brave. By noticing your grief, joining with others, and reaching out to offer comfort, you have taken at least a small step towards healing yourself and the world.

Such things such as depression or bereavement, grieving...Often the message is the message of the tree in winter. All the tree can do is wait — be quiet, wait, trust — and sooner or later the spring will come. I'm not saying that everything's just fine. Depressions are depressions — I have them too, and when I'm in the midst of them, all my good words, they don't help me either. All I can do is wait, and trust, and be silent. And that's a message, too.

— Brother David Steindl-Rast

Chapter 23: Self-Compassion[29]

> *A man cannot be comfortable without his own approval.* — Mark Twain

People are usually harder on themselves than they are on others. When we make a mistake or feel stressed out, we often respond with harsh self-criticism. This makes us feel isolated, unhappy, and even more stressed. Often, this leads to people simply avoiding new or challenging experiences for fearing of failing and eliciting a new wave of self-criticism. With self-compassion, instead of self-criticism, we give ourselves the same kindness and care we'd give to a good friend.

Kristin Neff is a self-compassion researcher, author, and associate professor in the University of Texas at Austin's department of educational psychology. She defines "self-compassion" as having three main components: mindfulness, a feeling of common humanity, and self-kindness.

Through mindfulness, we become aware of our own treatment of ourselves. Often, we do not even notice the harsh, critical tone of our own inner dialogues. Through a feeling of common humanity, we recognize that we ourselves are human and thus deserving of human empathy. The third element, self-kindness, requires the first two, and can be cultivated through intentional practices.

The practices here walk you through all three of those components.

The following practice asks you to notice the differences between the ways you typically treat the people you care about and the ways you typically treat yourself. It also asks you to consider why there may be differences between the two, and to contemplate what would happen if you treated yourself as compassionately as you treat others.

---

[29] Adapted from the Greater Good in Action website exercise, "Self-Compassion Break," http://ggia.berkeley.edu/practice/self_compassion_break

Greater Good in Action's Exercises were developed from author/researcher Kristin Neff's "Self-Compassion" concepts.

Practice: How Would You Treat a Friend?

STOP

Set aside 15 minutes to do this exercise. Stop whatever you are doing and devote your full attention to being still or slowing down. If it helps, close your eyes. Become conscious of your breath breathing itself. Follow one complete inhale-exhale cycle with your attention.

LOOK

First, think about times when a close friend feels really bad about him or herself or is really struggling in some way. How do you respond to your friend in these situations (if you're at your best)? Write down what you typically do and say, and note the tone in which you talk to your friend.

GO

Now think about times when you feel bad about yourself or are struggling. How do you typically respond to yourself in these situations? Write down what you typically do and say, and note the tone in which you talk to yourself.

_____

_____

_____

Did you notice a difference? If so, ask yourself why. What factors or fears come into play that leads you to treat yourself and others so differently?

_____

_____

_____

Write down how you think things might change if you responded to yourself when you're suffering in the same way you typically respond to a close friend.

_____

_____

_____

Now, move on to the next practice.

Practice: Self-Compassion Break

STOP

Set aside 15 minutes to do this exercise. Think of a situation in your life that is difficult. Call the situation to mind and see if you can actually feel the stress and emotional discomfort in your body.

LOOK

Now say to yourself, "This is a moment of suffering." This acknowledgment is a form of mindfulness — of simply noticing what is going on for you emotionally in the present moment, without judging that experience as good or bad. You can also say to yourself, "This hurts," or "This is stress." Use whatever statement feels most natural to you.

Next, say to yourself, "Suffering is a part of life." This is a recognition of your common humanity with others — that all people have trying experiences, and these experiences give you something in common with the rest of humanity rather than mark you as abnormal or deficient. Other options for this statement include "Other people feel this way," "I'm not alone," or "We all struggle in our lives."

GO

Now, put your hands over your heart, feel the warmth of your hands and the gentle touch on your chest, and say, "May I be kind to myself." This is a way to express self-kindness. You can also consider whether there is another specific phrase that would speak to you in that particular situation. Some examples: "May I give myself the compassion that I need," "May I accept myself as I am," "May I learn to accept myself as I am," "May I forgive myself," "May I be strong," and "May I be patient."

> How long will you suffer from the blows of a nonexistent hand?
> So come, return to the root of the root of your own soul.
> You are a ruby encased in granite.
> How long will you deceive us with this outer show?
> O friend, we can see the truth in your eyes!
> So come, return to the root of the root of your own soul.
>
> — *Rumi*

This practice can be used any time of day or night. If you practice it in moments of relative calm, it might become easier for you to experience the three parts of self-compassion — mindfulness, common humanity, and self-kindness — when you need them most.

Now let's go back to the first practice where you considered treating yourself as you would a friend — and put that into action with a self-compassionate letter.

Practice: Letter to Yourself

STOP
Set aside some time to write another letter. This one will be a letter to yourself.

LOOK
Think of an issue you have that tends to make you feel bad about yourself — a mistake, your appearance, etc. Imagine a friend who is unconditionally wise, loving, and compassionate. Imagine that this friend can see all your strengths and weaknesses, including what you don't like about yourself.

GO
Using the letter form provided on the following page, write a letter to yourself from the perspective of this imaginary friend, focusing on your perceived inadequacy. What would this friend say to you from a compassionate perspective? How might her suggestions embody care, encouragement, and support?

   If you prefer, you can write a letter as if you were talking to a dearly loved friend who was struggling with the same concern that you are. What words of compassion and support would you offer? Then go back and read the letter, applying the words to yourself.

Now wait. Put the letter down for a little while. Then come back to it and read it again, really letting the words sink in. Feel the compassion as it pours into you, soothing and comforting you. And may you continue to give yourself the same self-compassion in your day-to-day life.

Self-Compassion Studies*

In one study, the effectiveness of two exercises intended to help individuals experience self-compassion and optimism were compared to a control intervention. Individuals high in self-criticism were found to benefit noticeably from the two active exercises, experiencing significant increases in happiness.

Another self-compassion study examined self-compassion among adolescents. Findings suggest that self-compassion may be an effective intervention target for teens suffering from negative self-views.

---

* Leah B. Shapira & Myriam Mongrain, *"The benefits of self-compassion and optimism exercises for individual vulnerable to depression,"* The Journal of Positive Psychology.

Kristin D. Neff & Pittman McGehee, *"Self-Compassion and Psychological Resilience Among Adolescents and Young Adults"*

Letter of Gratitude

Dear _____

_____

_____

_____

_____

_____

_____

_____

_____

_____

_____

_____

_____

_____

_____

_____

_____

_____

_____

_____

_____

PART 4

Deepening Joy Through Gratitude

Chapter 25: Savoring Walk[30]

In our daily lives, we don't always notice or acknowledge the pleasant and positive things around us. As a result, we miss opportunities for positive experiences and positive emotions — the building blocks of long-term happiness. Research suggests that we can maximize the benefits of the good things around us by consciously savoring them rather than letting them pass us by or taking them for granted. This exercise offers one basic way to start savoring the bounty of goodness around us — not by going to some exotic destination, but by paying more careful attention to the sights, smells, and sounds we often neglect.

Participants who were encouraged to maintain a positive focus during daily walks for one week reported a greater increase in happiness at the end of the week, compared to participants who were encouraged to maintain a negative or neutral focus during their walks. Taking the time to "stop and smell the roses" — what researchers call "savoring" — can enhance happiness and boost feelings of appreciation and gratitude. Savoring helps us deepen the impact that positive events have on our emotional lives. Rather than just slipping from our awareness, or failing to register in the first place, these events sink into our minds and stay with us long after they are over. By becoming more attuned to our surroundings, we may also be more likely to connect with the people around us, even if it's just to share a smile.

[30] Adapted from the "Savoring Walk" exercise from the Greater Good in Action website, http://ggia.berkeley.edu/practice/savoring_walk#data-tab-how

Practice: Savoring Walk

STOP

Set aside 20 minutes to take a walk outside by yourself. You can still do this exercise in a light rain — provided you have a decent umbrella and rain jacket.

LOOK

As you walk, try to notice as many positive things around you as you can. These can be sights, sounds, smells, or other sensations. For example, you could focus on the breathtaking height of a tree you never really noticed before, the intricate architecture of a building on your block, the dance of sunshine off a window or puddle, the smell of grass or flowers, or the way other people look out for each other as they navigate crowded streets.

> *Be happy for this moment. This moment is your life.*
>
> — Omar Khayyam

As you notice each of these positive things, acknowledge each one in your mind — don't just let them slip past you. Pause for a moment as you hear or see each thing and make sure it registers with your conscious awareness, really taking it in. Try to identify what it is about that thing that makes it pleasurable to you.

> *Let the beauty of what you love be what you do. There are thousands of ways to kneel and kiss the ground.*
>
> — Rumi

GO

In the space below, write out three things you noticed on your savoring walk. If you wish, draw a picture of what you liked best.

_____

_____

_____

Chapter 26: The Beauty of Nature and its Gifts[31]

> *Those who contemplate the beauty of the Earth find reserves of strength that will endure as long as life lasts.*   — Rachel Carson

The beauties of nature are known to inspire spontaneous feelings of happiness, awe, and enjoyment. All of these things easily lead us to feel gratitude connected to nature. These feelings of thanks for nature's grandeur have spilled into poems, religious texts, paintings, sculptures, and songs for all of human history. In this chapter, we will explore cultivating this joyous feeling of thanks even further.

The following practice adapts the Savoring Walk from the previous chapter, to cultivate awareness of Nature as a gift.

[31] Practice: Savoring Nature Experience is inspired by the Savoring Walk practice from The Greater Good In Action website http://ggia.berkeley.edu/practice/savoring_walk

Practice: Savoring Nature

STOP

If you can, go to a place that you find particularly rich in natural beauty for this practice — but a simple walk in your own neighborhood will work too. Plan on spending at least twenty minutes immersed in nature, and if you are able to do so, use those twenty minutes to take a walk or hike. If you are unable to hike, you should still spend at least twenty minutes contemplating nature. Go to the most beautiful spot you can, even if it is just a small patch of flowers in your backyard.

LOOK

Just as you did when you were practicing the basic savoring walk, you will be trying to notice as many positive things around you as you can. Here, you will be focusing specifically on beautiful things around you that come from nature. These can be sights, sounds, smells, or other sensations. You might hear the sounds of birds or crickets, or feel the warm sun on your face, or the cool air near a waterfall or a lake. You may notice a lizard sunning itself, or a majestic cliff face. You may see the trees reaching up to the sky; each one is different, just like us.

> *If you will stay close to nature, to its simplicity, to the small things hardly noticeable, those things can unexpectedly become great and immeasurable.* — Maria Rilke

If you are in the city, savor the little pieces of nature that manage to thrive, despite all odds, in the urban environment. Look up at the sky and notice the formation of clouds or the fact that the sun is shining. Notice urban gardens, or plants that curl out of pavement in a vacant lot.

As you notice each of these positive natural things, acknowledge each one in your mind — don't just let them slip past you. Pause for a moment as you hear or see each thing and make sure it registers with your conscious awareness. Really take it in. Try to identify what it is about this part of nature that makes it pleasurable to you.

Now, before you move on, try thinking of this element of nature as a gift. Writing in this notebook, finish the following sentences, using three things you noticed as beautiful or pleasurable during your savoring nature walk.

Nature, thank you for:

_____

_____

_____

_____

Next, extend your awareness of nature past the sheer beauty of natural things to an awareness of the lifegiving gifts Nature bestows. Bring to your full awareness some of the things that Nature provides: the food you eat, the water you drink, and the air you breathe, as well as clothing, medicine, and other things crucial to your existence. Try thinking of these things, too, as gifts, rather than as givens.

> *Everything in life is a gift, and the appropriate response is Thank you.*
> — Brother David Steindl-Rast

Hanging on to this new awareness, write out some gifts from Nature that come to your mind. Focus on the things Nature gives you that enable you to stay alive. Name as many as you can think of.

I am grateful for nature's gifts of:

_____

_____

_____

_____

_____

GO

Consider the following statement from Dr. Robin Wall Kimmerer: "I've been told that my Potawatomi ancestors taught that the job of a human person is to learn, 'What can I give in return for the gifts of the Earth?'"

If you set out to learn the answer to this question, where would you start?

_____

_____

_____

What gifts do you have that you can share with the Earth?

_____

_____

_____

_____

_____

_____

_____

_____

What steps will you take today to give gifts to the Earth — to reciprocate the gifts of life, beauty, and endless variety that the Earth gives to you each day? For a list of some organizations devoted to helping the Earth, please view the appendix at the end of this book.

_____

_____

_____

_____

_____

_____

_____

_____

_____

_____

Chapter 27: Grateful Appreciation of The Arts[32]

There is within each one of us, personally, a realm of the artistic, in whatever way this might express itself — poetry or painting or music or in many less conspicuous ways. We are makers, "mindful makers," and within each one of us that realm of the artistic mediates between daily chores and spiritual aspirations. There is a passage that Gilbert Kerr, editor of the *Harvard Advocate,* wrote about W.H. Auden that might be a helpful text with which to start. Auden believed, said Kerr, that "a poet feels the impulse to create a work of art when the passive awe provoked by an event is transformed into a desire to express that awe in a rite of worship." He doesn't say "into a work of art." He says, "in a rite of worship." That rite of worship, in words, is poetry. In movement, it is dance. In color and line, it is painting.

> *What if imagination and art are not frosting at all, but the fountainhead of human experience?* — Rollo May

When we speak of art in this section, it's distinguished from crafts, which are primarily made for a practical purpose. With art, the emphasis is on meaning rather than purpose, on celebration rather than use of the thing made. This is a celebration, ultimately, of the superfluous. The superfluous is celebrated with the deep intuition that nothing is more important to us humans than the superfluous.

---

[32] Adapted from "The Artist at the Crux of Community," by Br. David Steindl-Rast on Gratefulness.org at http://www.gratefulness.org/resource/dsr-artist-at-crux/

and "Creative Expression," by Kristi Nelson on Gratefulness.org at http://www.gratefulness.org/area-of-interest/creative-expression/

Art, in its most expansive definition, contains all forms of creative expression. And creativity is one of the most potent forces in the world and in our lives. It is creativity which points us to new paths and new ways of seeing, and which offers us inspiration from both the inside and the outside.

Creative expression is rooted in the capacities for observation, discovery, imagination, and courage. It wakes us up, challenges us, and enriches all our lives. Those who dive deeply into a commitment to creative expression make their whole lives a canvas or a blank page onto which their hearts are poured . . . and our world is made better because of it.

> *When I hear music, I fear no danger. I am invulnerable. I see no foe. I am related to the earliest times, and to the latest.* — Henry David Thoreau

Art, no matter what its form, asks us to drop into stillness and to see what we see with new eyes, or hear with new ears. The nature of any successful artwork is to be a source of insight, inspiration, and joy with many levels to be explored. In the following practice we explore one beloved artwork.

Practice: Artwork Appreciation

> *A thing of beauty is a joy forever.*
> — John Keats

STOP

Select an artwork that means much to you. This could be a visual artwork, such as a painting, drawing, or sculpture. It could be a poem, or a recording of a song or instrumental piece that you particularly love.

What did you select?

_____

_____

_____

_____

_____

_____

LOOK

Each day, for three days, look or listen to whatever you chose. For instance, choose a poem that speaks to you and read it each day. Let it awaken a new experience each time you read it. Notice how no poem is the same poem twice if you read it with true presence.

In the space below, write down what you notice each day.

DAY ONE

_____

_____

_____

_____

_____

_____

DAY TWO

_____

_____

_____

_____

_____

_____

DAY THREE

_____

_____

_____

_____

_____

_____

_____

GO

Share the artwork with someone else. Read the poem to a friend. Show the painting you like to someone you think would get something from it. Make a music mix for a friend. Take note of your friend's experience with your chosen artwork. Did your friend see something in your chosen artwork that you also noticed? Did your friend see something entirely different?

How did it feel to share art with a friend?

Continue to take advantage of all of the wonderful art provided for your illumination and enjoyment.

Chapter 28: Looking at the World through the Eyes of a Child[33]

The typical circumstance of a child when seen in public these days is one of being dragged along by a long arm, while whoever is dragging the child is saying, "Come on, let's go! We don't have any time. We have to get home [or somewhere else]. Don't just stand there. Do something." But other cultures, many Native American tribes, for example, had an entirely different ideal for education: "A well-educated child ought to be able to sit and look when there is nothing to be seen," and "A well-educated child ought to be able to sit and listen when there is nothing to be heard."

— Brother David Steindl-Rast

We have all heard it said that childhood is too short to become the child you are meant to be. Fortunately, it's never too late. Right now, this beautiful child full of promise is there inside of you, just waiting to leap, skip, dance, and above all, look at every moment with fresh eyes.

In this practice, we will be deliberately looking at things the way a child might look at them. We will begin by meditating on a child's drawing. This is not idle playing, but a way of breaking out of your habitual ways of looking, or rather, not looking. The moment you really look, you find yourself surrounded by surprises. Surprise is always cause for gratefulness. And gratefulness gives you joy.

---

[33] Adapted from: "Strengthening Your Inner Child Through Gratefulness" formerly on Gratefulness.org

Quote from "The Monk In Us" by Brother David Steindl-Rast on Gratefulness.org at http://www.gratefulness.org/resource/dsr-the-monk-in-us/

Practice: Looking at the World Through a Child's Eyes

STOP and **LOOK**

Look at this child's picture of a tree. This is a tree when you were eight. Have you noticed its many colors? How firmly it grips the ground? How it reaches out towards the sky and especially towards the sun? And what a sun that is. It is reaching down: the tree and the sun are almost locking fingers. Take a deep, long look.

GO

Now, practice looking at something in real life, as if through the eyes of a child. Right now look at one thing in front of you. It doesn't matter whether it's a natural object or made by human hands. Don't just give it a name and file it in your mind as that name — really look at what it's made of. Look at its color with its different shades. Let your eyes caress its shape.

Now, imagine what it would be like if it were ten times this big. One hundred times this big. Or miniaturize it. Play with it. Make it alive, if it isn't already.

Make up your mind to look at a few more things with playful attention before the day is out.

On the next page, make a drawing — with crayons, if you have them — of one of the things you looked at through a child's eyes.

• • • • •

Conclude now with a little ritual. Rituals give strength to an experience. Just take a small piece of paper and write on it a name of endearment or nickname you liked as a child, a name by which no one has called you for a long time. Fold up the paper, carry it with you today, and remember: that child is singing within you.

> *Gratefulness unlocks joy. Nothing that we take for granted gives us joy. Yet the smallest surprise, received gratefully, yields a harvest of delight.*
> — Brother David Steindl-Rast

Chapter 29: Stop, Work, Flow: Work as Leisure[34]

We consider work and leisure opposites. But we all know that the best work is leisurely work, and if you don't work leisurely, you're in danger of knocking over with one hand what you're building up with the other.

What is the real opposite of work? Play. We have basically two kinds of activities, work and play. Work and play. Work has a clear purpose in mind, a goal, and when that purpose is achieved, the work as work is ended. In certain cases you cannot even continue; the very activity comes to an end when the purpose is achieved. For instance, when you are sewing on a button the purpose is to get it on to where you want. When it is sewn on, you can't sew it on any more.

Other activities that are work can continue after the purpose is achieved —for instance, vacuuming. The rug can look absolutely spotless, but say there is still a little spot somewhere and you vacuum again and then again. Sooner or later somebody's going to say, "Why are you playing around with this vacuum cleaner?" So from work, it turns into play — that kind of activity that doesn't need a purpose. It has all its meaning within itself and you can do it as long as you find it meaningful. If you answer, "It's very meaningful to me; I always dance with the vacuum cleaner on Monday nights," it may raise some eyebrows, but it's perfectly all right. Play does not have to achieve any purpose whatsoever.

---

[34] Adapted from "YES! With Thanks" by Brother David Steindl-Rast on Gratefulness.org
http://www.gratefulness.org/resource/yes-with-thanks/

So now we have purpose and meaning, two totally different things that we also get mixed up. Purpose is something that you manipulate your activity in order to achieve. Meaning gives itself to you. You would never say, "I took things in hand, kept them nicely under control, and achieved meaning." You don't achieve meaning that way; you achieve your purpose. When something becomes profoundly meaningful, you say, "It really did something to me, it grabbed me, it swept me off my feet, it knocked me over, it warmed my heart." Whatever it does to you, the more it does it, the more meaningful it is.

Where does leisure come in? It is the balance between work and play. Good work is playful work — work to which you have added what is best in play, namely doing it for its own sake and opening yourself so that meaning can flow into your activities. If we live and work in a leisurely manner, life becomes so much richer. Before you are leisurely, you can never be mindful. You're just running around like a chicken without a head. We do this most of the time; we're so busy, we don't have the time to breathe. But the moment we become leisurely, we allow ourselves the luxury of balancing work and play.

Balancing, by the way, means doing it at the same time. If you don't work leisurely, you can't spend your free time leisurely either. These days people have more and more free time and less and less leisure, because when their free time comes they are either so exhausted from their work that they simply collapse — or they are so in the groove of working that the only thing they can think of is doing a one-hour workout. The leisure never comes.

> *The supreme accomplishment is to blur the line between work and play.*
> — Arnold Toynbee

We are talking about a balance that is built in, balance between the clear purpose you are achieving and the meaning you are receiving. To the degree that you become mindful, you recognize that you are not doing so much but that it is all given to you.

Practice: A Leisurely Chore

STOP

The next time you have a sink full of dishes to wash, take a moment to breathe and focus your mind and your energy before you begin. In this practice, you will be learning how to approach an ordinary task with playful attention.

LOOK

Most people don't like washing dishes, but when they absolutely can't help it any more and the sink is filled to the brim, they get it over with. Yet millions of people in Japan go through courses every year to learn the Japanese tea ceremony, a very simple ritual which is basically preparing a cup of tea, serving it to a guest, and then washing the dishes in their presence, very simply and beautifully. One of the things they learn about serving tea is to lift all the light things — like the tiny little bamboo spoon for dishing out the tea — as if they were very heavy, and to lift all the heavy things, like the big kettle, as if they were featherweight.

GO

Keeping this technique in mind, wash your dishes. As you wash, pretend you are performing a tea ceremony for someone. Handle the heavy dishes as if they were very light. Lift all of the small forks and spoons as if they weighed ten pounds each. Focus on the movements of your hands as you wash, and see if you can view the motions of washings as you would view a ballet dancer practicing her art.

When you are done, reflect on the experience in writing. How was the experience of washing dishes different for you when you approached it with the artfulness of a tea ceremony?

_____

_____

_____

_____

_____

What are some other activities in your life that you can approach differently? Can you think of some ways to look at "tedious chores" in a new, playful way? What are some ways you can approach work as leisure?

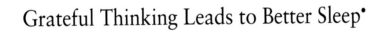

_____

_____

_____

_____

_____

_____

Leisurely living, even lifting things up in a mindful way, makes you mindful, and every activity becomes full of presence. Mindfulness leads immediately to gratefulness.

Grateful Thinking Leads to Better Sleep[*]

Researchers at the University of Manchester in England conducted a study to test whether individual differences in gratitude are related to sleep. They found that more grateful people slept longer and experienced a higher quality of uninterrupted rest. Participants in the study also reported feeling more refreshed upon waking.

_____

* "Gratitude influences sleep through the mechanism of pre-sleep cognitions," Wood AMI, Joseph S, Lloyd J, Atkins S. School of Psychology, University of Manchester, Manchester, England, UK

Chapter 30: Deepening Your Sense of Belonging[35]

In a culture that values independence, we sometimes forget that our survival and ability to thrive depend on interrelationships. In your mother's womb, you floated in the warm embrace of amniotic fluid and received a steady stream of nutrients through the umbilical cord. Perhaps you heard her sing lullabies to you then, so her voice became familiar before you were even born.

We not only depend on each other from the start, but we need also to treat our interdependence as the sacred gift it is. Whether we have been marvelously supported or terribly mistreated in the past (most of us experience a mix of each), we can now choose to live gratefully so that our sense of belonging grows ever stronger.

---

[35] Adapted from Gratefulness.org formerly on website.

Practice: Deepening Belonging

STOP

Close your eyes and feel the pulse of your heart. At this moment, your heart is sending blood to your lungs to receive oxygen and then to nourish every cell of your body through an intricate system of arteries. Equally amazing veins draw depleted blood back to your heart, where the cycle starts anew with each cycle of beats.

Here in our own hearts, then, lies a fundamental sacrament that all human beings (as well as many other creatures) have in common. Just as the nearness of the mother's heartbeat encourages her infant, our own heart brings us a certain assurance against loneliness. By its continual supply of sustenance, it supports our very lives. By beating in company with the hearts of others, it reveals us to be in relationship, even if we live alone in a farflung corner of the world. And by its rhythmic sympathy with the ocean waves, the cycles of seasons, the orbits of planets, it unites us with our world and worlds beyond us.

Can you feel this companionship now, in your own heart? Give yourself enough time to experience — rather than just think about — the degree to which you belong. A single stream of love unites the vast diversity of life in our universe.

LOOK

To which part of this vastness do you feel closest? You may think of another person, living or dead, but don't restrict yourself to human relationships if something else comes to mind: a woodpecker that visits your bird feeder every morning, a tulip poplar that lets you lean against its trunk when you're lonely, a stone you carry with you everywhere. "The world is charged with the

> *Extend the boundaries of the glowing kingdom of your love, gradually including your family, your neighbors, your community, your country, all countries — all living sentient creatures.*
> — Paramahansa Yogananda

grandeur of God," writes Gerard Manley Hopkins, and you can find friendship in the most unlikely places. You may even feel closest to an all-pervading Presence that goes by many names and yet again is beyond naming. (Don't think any less of your choice if it's not human. The more aware you become of the living nature of our entire Earth, the better you'll be able to heal the alienation that allows people to exploit Her.)

GO

Write down the name (or, if a name isn't appropriate, a reminder) of the one you've chosen. Now let all the goodness of this relationship flood into your heart. What have you received from this friend, for which you're grateful? What have you given? Your ability to give is, of course, part of the continuum of gratitude as well. Gifts flow to you and also through you to others. As you enter into this give-and-take, you enter a universe gracefilled and fully alive.

Clearly name the gifts you receive through your friendship, and the gifts you give through your friendship.

_____

_____

_____

_____

_____

_____

_____

_____

Now, go one step further and ponder the gift your friend is, in and of himself or herself. You may feel joyful while doing this exercise, but it's also okay to feel sad — for instance, if the person closest to you has passed on. Just bear in mind that the sadness is directly related to the extent of your love. No matter what, you can hold onto the gift of love between you and another. Love is an indestructible power. Allow yourself to feel that power of love for a little while before going on.

Congratulations! Every time you gratefully appreciate a friend or loved one, as you did today, you build a more peaceful, loving community on Earth.

Chapter 31: Random Acts of Kindness: Gratefulness Among Strangers[36]

In his essay, "How Big is Your Family?" Brother David Steindl-Rast discusses the modern reluctance to express authentic gratitude to those we don't know well. Brother David says: "Bonds are established when you say thank you. You enter into obligation. Nowadays we don't like obligations. When I learned English sixty-five years or so ago, one could still say "very much obliged" instead of "thank you." In America you can't say "very much obliged" because nobody wants to be very much obliged. When people move into a new neighborhood they say, 'Let's not start giftgiving with our neighbors, it just creates obligations,' as if this were something unpleasant."

Try the following two practices this week to extend gratitude toward people you come into contact with, and explore the feeling of this kind of connection with a stranger.

[36] Adapted from the Greater Good In Action website exercise, "Random Acts of Kindness," at http://ggia.berkeley.edu/practice/random_acts_of_kindness

and the essay "Three Strategies for Bringing More Kindness into Your Life," Juliane Breines, at http://greatergood.berkeley.edu/article/item/three_strategies_for_bringing_more_kindness_into_your_life

Practice: Thank a Stranger

STOP

Decide that sometime this week, you will thank a stranger, with sincere appreciation, for something he or she does for you.

LOOK

Be on the lookout for an act that makes you grateful. This could be a onetime occurrence, such as a stranger holding a door for you, giving you the right of way, or giving you directions. It could be something that happens regularly; you may want to say thank you to a person who is not a total stranger, but who is not in your circle of actual friends — such as the person that makes your coffee or changes the oil in your car. You could also express your gratefulness for an action not directed specifically at yourself; for instance, you might observe someone picking up trash at the beach and feel grateful that this person cares enough to help our environment.

GO

With sincere appreciation, acknowledge with a wave, or tell the person why their actions are meaningful to you. Thank them for the specific things that they've done which make you feel grateful.

> *No act of kindness, no matter how small, is ever wasted.*
> — Aesop

In the next practice, you will be selecting one day this week to perform five acts of kindness — all five in one day. It doesn't matter if the acts are big or small, but it is more effective if you perform a variety of acts.

The acts do not need to be for the same person; the person doesn't even have to be aware of them. Examples include feeding a stranger's parking meter, donating blood, helping a friend with a chore, or providing a meal to a person in need.

Practice: Random Acts of Kindness

STOP

Select a day to be your Random Acts of Kindness day. The first time you perform this practice, you may want to select a day when you don't feel too pressed for time or overloaded with work. (Later, however, you may want to specifically try it again when you feel overloaded. This practice, paradoxically, reduces stress and takes you out of your focused anxiety.)

> *The best way to cheer yourself up is to cheer somebody else up.*
> — Mark Twain

> *It is not what you gather, but what you scatter, that tells what kind of life you have lived.*
> — Anonymous

LOOK

Be on the lookout for spontaneous Random Acts of Kindness you can perform. It can be a smile or compliment to someone you don't know. You will probably also need to create some from scratch — donate your time to a volunteer organization or help a friend with something.

GO

Write down what you did in at least one or two sentences. What were the results? How do you think your action impacted the other person? And how did it make you feel?

_____

_____

_____

_____

_____

The Helper's High*

Psychologists have identified a typical state of euphoria reported by those engaged in charitable activity. They call it "helper's high," and it's based on the theory that giving produces endorphins in the brain.

At Emory University, a study revealed that helping others lit up the same part of the brain as receiving rewards or experiencing pleasure.

Research at the National Institutes of Health showed that the same area of the brain that is activated in response to food or sex (namely, pleasure), lit up when the participants in the study throught about giving money to a charity.

According to the results of the "Social Capital Community Benchmark Survey," overseen by researchers from Harvard University, those who gave contributions of time or money were "42 percent more likely to be happy" than those who didn't give.

---

* James Baraz and Shoshana Alexander, "The Helper's High," from the Greater Good Science Center website.

PART 5

Many Thanks

Chapter 32: Using Stop, Look, Go to Create Your Own Practices

At the beginning of this workbook, we mentioned that keeping a gratitude journal is one of the best ways to cultivate gratitude. It's our hope that the writing exercises in this workbook are just the beginning, and that you will continue to keep a gratitude journal of your own.

You have also experimented with a number of other ways to cultivate gratefulness. Taking a savoring walk, thanking a loved one, walking a virtual labyrinth, drawing a picture, meditating, creating a "thanks jar," practicing random acts of kindness... as you have seen, gratefulness can be cultivated in any number of active ways.

Looking back at all of the practices in this workbook, can you name three that particularly resonated with you? Try not to overthink this question; instead, quickly pick the three practices that jump out as having a lasting impact.

_____

_____

_____

Now look back at the three practices you chose. Can you find a common thread among them? Some people find that writing things out has the most impact. Others find visually creative projects impact them the most, and still others are most

> *There are multiple ways to practice the strategy of gratitude, and it would be wise to choose what works best for you. When the strategy loses its freshness or meaningfulness, don't hesitate to make a change in how, when and how often you express yourself.*
> — Sonja Lyubomirsky, from *The How of Happiness: A New Approach to Getting the Life You Want*

affected by social interactions. Some are most deeply affected by pure meditation, and others prefer physical actions such as taking a walk. Knowing what affects you deeply can help you create more effective practices for yourself in the future.

In this workbook, we have used the STOP, LOOK, GO framework to create many different kinds of gratitude practices. Naturally, we focused on practices that were as universal as possible. One advantage to creating your own practices is that you can create ones that are very specific to your own particular life.

Can you think of a practice that you would like to create? Think about something you do regularly that requires you to utilize a learned skill or art with deep focus and awareness. Pick whatever you feel is most appropriate; it could be your profession, an art form, a sport, charity work, teaching, crafts, planting a garden, or anything else that seems like a good fit for this practice.

Write the practice as if you are writing out instructions to someone else. Use your deep knowledge of the subject you chose to make it as detailed and passionate as you can.

As you write, refer to the basic steps of STOP, LOOK, GO.

STOP: Become present, awake. and aware.

LOOK: Notice, observe, consider, have a direct experience.

GO: Acknowledge, take action, express, and commit to doing something with the opportunity that life presents to you.

Practice: Create Your Own Practice

STOP

Think of something specific to your own life and experiences that you would love to explore with a gratitude practice. This could be a particular job that you do regularly, a talent you wish to accentuate, or conversely, something you consider yourself to be not-so-good at doing and wish to improve. It could be a perception you wish to explore, or an experience you want to deepen. Your practice could revolve around a specific person in your life, or a place you go regularly. One woman, for instance, wrote a practice specifically for people who practice massage and other healing therapies.

When you have finished deciding on what your practice will be about, give it a title.

TITLE OF YOUR PRACTICE:

_____

LOOK

Take your time thinking about ways that can deepen your awareness and insight about your chosen theme. Notice any emotions that surface as you examine this facet of your life more closely. In the space below, write down instructions, as if for someone else, for closely observing and considering this facet of your life. How can you engage with it more directly?

_____

_____

_____

GO

In response to your observations, think of specific actions you can take to engage yourself in a concrete, physical way. In this workbook, you have been asked to create a drawing, a collage, or other artwork; write in your journal; interact and share with a friend or a stranger; take a walk. Feel free to use any of these activities that make sense for your practice, or use your imagination to create something completely new. If your practice concerns a specific activity, you could simply perform this activity with full mindfulness and engagement. Regardless of what you choose, write specific instructions about taking action.

_____

_____

_____

_____

When you are finished writing about the practice, take a break from it. Tomorrow, come back and read what you've written. Then, try out your own practice.

Below, write out a response to your experience with your own practice. Did you learn anything unexpected?

_____

_____

_____

_____

How did your own words resonate?

_____

_____

_____

_____

How effective was your practice?

_____

_____

_____

_____

How would you compare it to practices you've done in the past?

_____

_____

_____

_____

Congratulations! You have just created your own grateful living practice! Now, it's time to create some more. Choose at least one of the basic themes below as a starting point for your second personal grateful living practice. If you wish, do all of them!

- Create a special practice for treasuring your closest loved ones.
- Create a practice that helps you give to others in whatever way you in particular choose to give back to the world.
- Create a practice unique to yourself that unlocks happiness, joy, and appreciation of daily moments in your life.
- Create a practice for coping with difficult moments.

What are some practices you want to create?

_____

_____

_____

_____

_____

_____

_____

_____

_____

_____

_____

_____

_____

_____

Chapter 33: More Daily Grateful Living Practice Ideas[37]

Here are 30 more grateful living practices for you to try. These practices range from actions that will take you only a moment to those that will take a larger commitment of your time. If there is one practice on this list that you would like to try every day, do so. Or try a new one each day. Or switch it up.

> *Enjoy the energy boost grateful living gives you. Dare to tackle new projects. Taste the joy of turning feeling good into doing good.*
> — Brother David Steindl-Rast

What matters is that you do something every day to build the habit of intentionally directing your attention to notice and appreciate the gifts of your life.

[37] Adapted from "Daily Grateful Living Practice Ideas" on Gratefulness.org http://www. gratefulness.org/resource/practice-ideas/

30 Daily Grateful Living Practice Ideas

1. Every night before you go to sleep, take an inventory of the things for which you are grateful. Let them percolate through your mind and calm your body. Write down at least five things that matter to you.

2. At any point during the day, reflect upon one important thing that you have learned that day. Write down what you have learned.

3. Send a card or an e-card, letting someone know that you are thinking of them today. Expect nothing in return. Just share your appreciation and acknowledgement.

4. Sit quietly and allow a sense of peace to enter your heart. From this place, light a candle in your space. Create a grateful intention and settle into the peace of residing in gratefulness for a few, precious moments.

5. Start your day with an intention to show up absolutely, wholeheartedly to everything you do today. Notice at the end of the day if anything changed because of this intention.

6. Make the decision to see your most challenging moments today as opportunities. What might be making itself known or available to you in hard times? How can you cultivate even small sentiments of gratefulness for the gifts that come from struggle? Reflect on this at the beginning and the end of the day.

7. Turn all of the "waiting" moments of the day into moments of heightened awareness. Try to be fully present in these moments to what might be blessings in disguise. Notice that the time "between" things is a huge gift. Enjoy the gift.

8. If you share a meal with others today, before or while you eat, ask each person to share something for which they are grateful. If you are eating alone, bring to mind something for which you are grateful and dedicate your meal to that "great fullness."

9. Notice your hands. Think of all they do for you. Can you imagine what it would be like to offer them your true appreciation at a host of moments each day? Notice how much they help to facilitate what you love in life. Take care of them.

10. Reach out to someone you know is going through a difficult time. You do not have to have the right things to say, just connect in a meaningful way.

11. Before you eat, take a moment to feel grateful to all those who contributed to creating your meal: the farmer who grew the vegetables, the hens that laid the eggs, the workers who harvested the wheat and stocked the food, etc.

12. Make a list of grateful poems, and share them with a friend.

13. Make a playlist of grateful songs. Listen to it when you wake up in the morning. Have a dance party with a friend.

14. While racing somewhere, take 30 seconds to stop, take a breath, and look at the sky or at the environment around you. What was begging for your attention?

15. Do something truly generous for someone else today. Expand into your most full-blown expression of generosity. Give as if your life depended on it, and then try giving a little more. Stretch into your capacity. Seek nothing in return.

16. Tell someone whom you love that you love them — and offer that comment a larger context by spelling out some of the reasons why you are grateful for them.

17. Ask someone a sincere question. There is hardly a more precious gift than true inquiry and deep listening.

18. Make a financial contribution to a non-profit organization engaged in work that you value. Accompany that gift with a note of appreciation for how hard they are working to advance missions in which you believe. Feel interconnected.

19. Support the arts by purchasing a book; downloading music and paying for it; buying a painting, drawing, or sculpture; getting a ticket for a live performance; or otherwise contributing to an artist you enjoy.

20. Ask yourself: "What is the opportunity for gratefulness in this moment?" Try this when things are not going as you had planned.

21. Give someone a grateful hug. Actually give the hug — don't take a hug. Ask first.

22. Pick out five things that you do not need anymore, and give them away with joy.

23. Put a bag in your pocket, go for a walk, and make a corner of the world more beautiful by picking up the litter along the way. Your appreciation of the earth will be contagious to others.

24. Quick! Without too much thinking, make a list of ten things you love about yourself.

_____

_____

_____

_____

_____

_____

_____

_____

_____

_____

25. Watch Brother David's video, "A Good Day." Share it with a friend.

26. Incorporate gratitude into your exercise routine.

27. Bring to mind someone for whom you are grateful. Savor this image or memory. Try to allow the image to be held by all the cells of your body, not just in your mind. Notice what happens in your emotions and body when you do this.

28. Ask yourself, "What has surpassed my expectations in life?"

29. Have a potluck "Gratefulness party." Invite each of your friends to share something he or she is grateful for.

30. Worldwide, 775 million people are illiterate. Feel your good fortune as you read this sentence, and as you read anything today.

Gratitude Journal

Gratitude Journal

_____

_____

_____

_____

_____

_____

_____

_____

_____

_____

_____

_____

_____

_____

_____

_____

_____

_____

_____

_____

_____

Gratitude Journal

Gratitude Journal

_____

_____

_____

_____

_____

_____

_____

_____

_____

_____

_____

_____

_____

_____

_____

_____

_____

_____

_____

Gratitude Journal

_____

_____

_____

_____

_____

_____

_____

_____

_____

_____

_____

_____

_____

_____

_____

_____

_____

_____

_____

_____

_____

Gratitude Journal

_____

_____

_____

_____

_____

_____

_____

_____

_____

_____

_____

_____

_____

_____

_____

_____

_____

_____

_____

_____

_____

Gratitude Journal

Gratitude Journal

_____

_____

_____

_____

_____

_____

_____

_____

_____

_____

_____

_____

_____

_____

_____

_____

_____

_____

_____

_____

_____

_____

Gratitude Journal

_____

_____

_____

_____

_____

_____

_____

_____

_____

_____

_____

_____

_____

_____

_____

_____

_____

_____

_____

_____

Gratitude Journal

_____

_____

_____

_____

_____

_____

_____

_____

_____

_____

_____

_____

_____

_____

_____

_____

_____

_____

_____

_____

_____

Gratitude Journal

_____

_____

_____

_____

_____

_____

_____

_____

_____

_____

_____

_____

_____

_____

_____

_____

_____

_____

_____

_____

_____

Gratitude Journal

_____

_____

_____

_____

_____

_____

_____

_____

_____

_____

_____

_____

_____

_____

_____

_____

_____

_____

_____

_____

Gratitude Journal

_____

_____

_____

_____

_____

_____

_____

_____

_____

_____

_____

_____

_____

_____

_____

_____

_____

_____

_____

_____

Gratitude Journal

_____

_____

_____

_____

_____

_____

_____

_____

_____

_____

_____

_____

_____

_____

_____

_____

_____

_____

_____

_____

_____

Gratitude Journal

_____

_____

_____

_____

_____

_____

_____

_____

_____

_____

_____

_____

_____

_____

_____

_____

_____

_____

_____

_____

_____

Gratitude Journal

_____

_____

_____

_____

_____

_____

_____

_____

_____

_____

_____

_____

_____

_____

_____

_____

_____

_____

_____

Gratitude Journal

_____

_____

_____

_____

_____

_____

_____

_____

_____

_____

_____

_____

_____

_____

_____

_____

_____

_____

_____

_____

_____

_____

Gratitude Journal

_____

_____

_____

_____

_____

_____

_____

_____

_____

_____

_____

_____

_____

_____

_____

_____

_____

_____

_____

_____

_____

_____

Gratitude Journal

Gratitude Journal

_____

_____

_____

_____

_____

_____

_____

_____

_____

_____

_____

_____

_____

_____

_____

_____

_____

_____

_____

_____

Gratitude Journal

Gratitude Journal

_____

_____

_____

_____

_____

_____

_____

_____

_____

_____

_____

_____

_____

_____

_____

_____

_____

_____

_____

_____

Gratitude Journal

Gratitude Journal

_____

_____

_____

_____

_____

_____

_____

_____

_____

_____

_____

_____

_____

_____

_____

_____

_____

_____

_____

_____

_____

_____

Gratitude Journal

Gratitude Journal

_____

_____

_____

_____

_____

_____

_____

_____

_____

_____

_____

_____

_____

_____

_____

_____

_____

_____

_____

_____

Gratitude Journal

Gratitude Journal

_____

_____

_____

_____

_____

_____

_____

_____

_____

_____

_____

_____

_____

_____

_____

_____

_____

_____

_____

_____

Gratitude Journal

_____

_____

_____

_____

_____

_____

_____

_____

_____

_____

_____

_____

_____

_____

_____

_____

_____

_____

_____

_____

_____

_____

_____

_____

Gratitude Journal

_____

_____

_____

_____

_____

_____

_____

_____

_____

_____

_____

_____

_____

_____

_____

_____

_____

_____

_____

_____

Gratitude Journal

Gratitude Journal

_____

_____

_____

_____

_____

_____

_____

_____

_____

_____

_____

_____

_____

_____

_____

_____

_____

_____

_____

Gratitude Journal

Gratitude Journal

_____

_____

_____

_____

_____

_____

_____

_____

_____

_____

_____

_____

_____

_____

_____

_____

_____

_____

_____

_____

_____

_____

Gratitude Journal

Gratitude Journal

_____

_____

_____

_____

_____

_____

_____

_____

_____

_____

_____

_____

_____

_____

_____

_____

_____

_____

_____

_____

_____

Gratitude Journal

_____

_____

_____

_____

_____

_____

_____

_____

_____

_____

_____

_____

_____

_____

_____

_____

_____

_____

_____

_____

_____

Gratitude Journal

_____

_____

_____

_____

_____

_____

_____

_____

_____

_____

_____

_____

_____

_____

_____

_____

_____

_____

_____

_____

Gratitude Journal

_____

_____

_____

_____

_____

_____

_____

_____

_____

_____

_____

_____

_____

_____

_____

_____

_____

_____

_____

To The Reader

This is a limited edition of

STOP — LOOK — GO: A Grateful Practice Workbook

and we want your feedback.

We will incorporate your suggestions and

criticisms in the next edition of the book.

Please write to us at stoplookgobook@gmail.com

We look forward to hearing from you.

In addition, we hope that you will enjoy these practices so much

that you will be inspired to create some new practices to share with us.

Thank you. Together we are making the world a more grateful place.

Sincerely,

Gary Fiedel

When you have hope you actually create a memory of the future that your mind starts working toward.

— Marsha Huber

Acknowledgments

By Gary Fiedel

To **Karie Jacobson** for saying yes to creating this workbook. She researched and selected the best practices, organized them into a logical order, rewrote them to fit into the Stop-Look-Go format, and selected quotes and science facts to augment the text. She took an idea I have had for many years and made it manifest.

To **Joan Lazarus**, a dear friend and talented artist, who designed every page of this book to make it clear to read and easy to write in. Her enthusiasm and creative input make this book a delight.

To **A Network for Grateful Living**, (ANG*L) – www.gratefulness.org… From the day 16 years ago when Brother David brought together Terry Pearce, Daniel Uvanovic and me to create a website focusing on gratitude. I have watched this organization grow. What began as just a website has become an international movement dedicated to spreading grateful living to all. I especially want to thank our founding board members Tom and Nancy Driscoll, Lynne Twist, Roshi Joan Halifax and Mike Lippit whose vision and dedication launched the website into the world. And the vision continues to expand under the current leadership of the Board and Staff. My deep appreciation to all.

The **Greater Good Science Center**, www.greatergood.berkeley.edu – I want to thank them for all the scientific work they have done showing the positive effects of gratitude in one's life. For their generous permission to us to use practices and information from their website for this book. Their website is a treasured resource.

To **Candice Fuhrman**…My wife and the love of my life who happens to know more about books than any person I have ever met. Her guidance and inspiration has influenced this book from cover to cover. Her ongoing input and encouragement has made this book a reality.